PRACTICAL SOCIAL WORK

Series Editor: Jo Campling

(BASW)

Social work is at an important stage in its development. All professions must be responsive to changing social and economic conditions if they are to meet the needs of those they serve. This series focuses on sound practice and the specific contribution which social workers can make to the well-being of our society in the 1990s.

The British Association of Social Workers has always been conscious of its role in setting guidelines for practice and in seeking to raise professional standards. The conception of the Practical Social Work series arose from a survey of BASW members to discover where they, the practitioners in social work, felt there was the most need for new literature. The response was overwhelming and enthusiastic, and the result is a carefully planned, coherent series of books. The emphasis is firmly on practice, set in a theoretical framework. The books will inform, stimulate and promote discussion, thus adding to the further development of skills and high professional standards. All the authors are practitioners and teachers of social work, representing a wide variety of experience.

JO CAMPLING

Robert Adams
Self-Help, Social Work and Empowerment

David Anderson
Social Work and Mental Handicap

Robert Brown, Stanley Bute and Peter Ford
Social Workers at Risk

Alan Butler and Colin Pritchard
Social Work and Mental Illness

Roger Clough
Residential Work

David M. Cooper and David Ball
Social Work and Child Abuse

Veronica Coulshed
Management in Social Work

Veronica Coulshed
Social Work Practice: An introduction (2nd edn)

Paul Daniel and John Wheeler
Social Work and Local Politics

Peter R. Day
Sociology in Social Work Practice

Lena Dominelli
Anti-Racist Social Work:
A Challenge for White Practitioners and Educators

Celia Doyle
Working with Abused Children

Geoff Fimister
Welfare Rights Work in Social Services

Kathy Ford and Alan Jones
Student Supervision

Alison Froggatt
Family Work with Elderly People

Danya Glaser and Stephen Frosh
Child Sexual Abuse

Gill Gorell Barnes
Working with Families

Jalna Hanmer and Daphne Statham
Women and Social Work:
Towards a Woman-Centred Practice

Tony Jeffs and Mark Smith
Youth Work

Michael Kerfoot and Alan Butler
Problems of Childhood and Adolescence

Mary Marshall
Social Work with Old People (2nd edn)

Paula Nicolson and Rowan Bayne
Applied Psychology for Social Workers (2nd edn)

Kieran O'Hagan
Crisis Intervention in Social Services

Michael Oliver
Social Work with Disabled People

Lisa Parkinson
Separation, Divorce and Families

Malcolm Payne
Social Care in the Community

Malcolm Payne
Working in Teams

John Pitts
Working with Young Offenders

Michael Preston-Shoot
Effective Groupwork

Carole R. Smith
Adoption and Fostering: Why and How

Carole R. Smith
Social Work with the Dying
and Bereaved

Carole R. Smith, Mary T. Lane and
Terry Walshe
Child Care and the Courts

Alan Twelvetrees
Community Work (2nd edn)

Hilary Walker and Bill Beaumont (eds)
Working with Offenders

FORTHCOMING TITLES

Jim Barber
Social Work Practice

Lynne Berry, Crescy Cannan and Karen Lyons
Social Work in Europe

Suzy Braye and Michael Preston-Shoot
Practising Social Work Law

Suzy Croft and Peter Beresford
Involving the Consumer

Angela Everitt et al
Applied Research for Better Practice

Michael Freeman
The Children's Act 1989

David Hebblewhite and Tom Leckie
Social Work with Addictions

Paul Henderson and David Francis
Working with Rural Communities

Rosemary Jefferson and Mike Shooter
Preparing for Practice

Jeremy Kearney and Dave Evans
A Systems Approach to Social Work

Joyce Lishman
Communication and Social Work

Carole Lupton (ed)
Working with Violence

Graham McBeath and Stephen Webb
The Politics of Social Work

Ruth Popplestone and Cordelia Grimwood
Women and Management

Steven Shardlow
Practice: Learning and Teaching

Gill Stewart and John Stewart
Social Work and Housing

Sociology in Social Work Practice

Peter R. Day

QUARLES

MACMILLAN

First published 1987 by
THE MACMILLAN PRESS LTD
Houndmills, Basingstoke, Hampshire RG21 2XS
and London
Companies and representatives
throughout the world

ISBN 0–333–38556–X hardcover
ISBN 0–333–38557–8 paperback

A catalogue record for this book is available
from the British Library.

Printed in Great Britain by
Antony Rowe Ltd
Chippenham, Wiltshire

Reprinted 1990, 1992 (twice)

Series Standing Order

If you would like to receive future titles in this series as they are published, you can
make use of our standing order facility. To place a standing order please contact your
bookseller or, in case of difficulty,write to us at the address below with your name
and address and the name of the series. Please state with which title you wish to
begin your standing order. (If you live outside the United Kingdom we may not have
the rights for your area, in which case we will forward your order to the publisher
concerned.)

Customer Services Department, Macmillan Distribution Ltd
Houndmills, Basingstoke, Hampshire RG21 2XS, England

Contents

vi   *Contents*

Acknowledgements

I would like to thank the people who have helped with this book in a variety of ways. I am thinking of users or clients of social services, social workers, students and social work teachers who have shared their experiences and ideas and with whom it has been stimulating to discuss aspects of social work which are often taken for granted. Paul Armstrong, Clive Coleman, Vic Rhodes and Wilf Attenborough have been tolerant and constructive critics but cannot be held responsible for the result. Jean Steel, Heather Clarke and Pat Moody have given secretarial and administrative support, and Val Hurst gave invaluable help in completing the work.

Peter R. Day

1

Perspectives and Methods in Sociology

This chapter introduces the main themes of the book. It begins with a discussion of the relevance and usefulness of sociology in social work practice and what social workers should derive from studying it. This leads to an examination of the relationship between theory and practice in social work and different sociological approaches. At the end of the chapter I outline the way the rest of the book is organised.

Sociology and social work

Social work is carried on in society, so that a social worker can never be a wholly independent or isolated agent. The very existence of social work and the activities of its practitioners reflect the fact that social workers operate within social systems. It is therefore inescapable that understanding sociology should help social workers to make a more effective contribution to their clients' welfare and to society. But it would be misleading to suggest that there is a single uniform set of methods and theories known as sociology which provides the whole truth about social life and social problems. A moment's reflection shows that if we had reached that situation there would be no further need for open-ended enquiry. What is argued here is that sociology provides a number of viewpoints or perspectives on social life which are useful in developing greater understanding to guide intervention (or non-intervention).

People who are referred or who refer themselves to

1

probation or social services departments often represent at an individual or family level social problems of wider society such as racial tensions, unemployment, industrial conflict, poverty and delinquency. There are also people who have problems in coping in social life because of drug dependence, problems of personal identity, mental illness and physical and mental disability. This wide variety of problems and needs gives rise to anomalies and strains in relationships between people in society. Individuals may be seen as 'problems' for 'society' or by 'society' and for many people society itself is seen as the problem or the source of their pain and distress. Social services and social workers are part of what is often a confusing and anxiety-provoking picture: their roles may themselves be problematic. But we may say at this stage that the state undertakes some responsibility to deal with some problems and needs and social workers, often employed by the state, give personal attention to people who have special difficulties or who do not 'fit in'. Sociological analysis is important because the kinds of jobs social workers do are closely associated with, and usually derive from the social structure. This may be illustrated by reference to the observation that social structures do not treat people equally. Groups of people are commonly distinguished by criteria such as size, ethnicity, age, sex, and physical characteristics and the presence or absence of deficits or handicaps. Criteria like these may be used to rank people to form different kinds of hierarchies on the basis of access to resources. People with access to resources usually have power or the ability to enforce their will on others. Powerful people control the decision-making about how resources will be distributed. Those with power have more control over and access to economic processes. They have more goods and services as well as decision-making power to protect their privileged position. By contrast, the poor have little money and limited ability to get the resources they need and they experience higher rates of social isolation, unemployment, lower levels of schooling, and more disease and crime. Membership of minority groups (for example, the poor, the elderly, some ethnic groups, and the handicapped) increases the likelihood that your access to resources will be limited.

Most of the people known to social workers come from the poorest and least educated groups in the community and social workers often have to deal with the consequences of social policies, for example relating to employment, housing, crime and sickness. It seems reasonable, then, to argue that in their training and education social workers should learn about social structure and about social problems including the ones mentioned here. Different sociological perspectives provide useful insights into the 'problems' and 'needs' that confront social workers. So far it has been argued that sociology is useful to social workers in partly explaining social structure and problems and issues in social life. I have said that it is useful in studying large-scale problems like unemployment and poverty thus indicating some of the limits to social work intervention. It is also about people in groups and as individuals who live in a social context which influences them in a wide variety of ways. Membership of social groups affects peoples' opportunities in relation to employment, education, health care and welfare services. Sociological research is also of help to social workers in understanding processes of change and development in small groups which are an important setting for practice. Most people are involved in a variety of groups in their daily lives and they are essential to meeting many individual and social needs. Many of the personal needs of individuals are met in an informal way by families and resources in peoples' neighbourhoods. These informal caring networks often provide a great deal of help, although it has to be recognised that these resources vary greatly. For example, one family may apparently cope well with problems or needs which for another are very stressful or burdensome. Social workers need to have some knowledge of the networks of which people form a part or of possible networks which they might join. However, the study of sociology suggests a need for caution. In community-based models of social work the most vulnerable, disadvantaged and stigmatised people could be at risk as they offend local norms of behaviour and are often rejected by their local communities.

The sociological study of organisations contributes to understanding their objectives and structures, and how they change. The organisational aspects of social work are of increasing significance and play a more important part in influencing the provision of service than is sometimes recognised. Sociological research has led to greater awareness of the structural and organisational situations of clients and social workers and their responses to them and to each other. Sociology contributes to social workers' interests and concerns on various levels. I have referred to larger aspects of social structure such as economic and governmental institutions in which human relationships may seem impersonal and remote. But the smaller, more intimate aspects of society only fully make some kind of sense if they are understood against the background of the macro-world. In turn the macro-world has little reality for people unless it is repeatedly represented in face-to-face relationships in the micro-world. Our understanding of our immediate face-to-face relationships with others is dependent on the wider social context. Both social levels depend on the other for their meaning and both are essential to our experience of society. Many processes between individuals depend on social structures, conventions, rules and language. For example, in understanding how people become acquainted or isolated it is necessary to pay attention to larger issues and problems to understand the finer texture of relationships. Interaction takes place on a symbolic meaningful level and individuals and groups vary according to the meanings which are attached to behaviour and relationships. Sociology is of help in scrutinising aspects of relationships like these which are often taken for granted as much by social workers as any other people. One hallmark of sociological consciousness is the ability to look at a situation from the viewpoints of different people and this seems to be a major contributuion to understanding social work.

I have said that various 'problems' and 'needs' are presented to social workers. By placing these words in inverted commas I am indicating that, from a sociological point of view these ideas are problematic. There are various views on how 'problems' or 'needs' are defined and, having defined them, on what should be done about them. Ideas about social action are related to assumptions about the nature of behaviour and 'society' and sociological analysis contributes to understanding of the values of different individuals and groups which may be taken for granted. Sociologists study values as constituents of social structure and culture, and examine the meaning and function of group and social values. They usefully question to what extent social workers share values and whether they have a dominant ideology, for example. This questioning of basic assumptions is useful in that it may challenge ways of working with clients of social agencies and the role of political and organisational influences on them. Social scientists generally are aware of the philosophical and ethical implications of their own work as well as the implications of the activities of people like lawyers and social workers.

The notion of 'society' is ambiguous: it may refer to the government, or to various influential groups who may have very different views about any given social issue. Social workers experience this ambiguity in the very mixed attitudes that are held towards people who deviate from social norms and it is seen in expectations that social workers will act as society's 'protectors' as well as society's conscience. Social work itself is an institution of considerable importance in society. By looking beyond official versions or commonly-accepted accounts of action sociologists often teach us that a 'problem' to one group of people may be seen as routine or normal to another. It leads to increased awareness that human events have different levels of meaning, some of which may be hidden from consciousness. Sociology is a discipline which will always seem a threat to those who claim to have the single correct vision of 'social reality' and who do not want to or cannot cope with open-ended and even apparently irreverent discussion of social life. They raise serious questions about statements beginning 'of course', such as 'Of course all our decisions are made democratically in this group' and 'Of course these kids are delinquent because of the telly'. The 'problem' of democratic leadership as seen by the team leader may not be the first sociological problem, which may be how the team works at all. Concentration on 'delinquency' or on 'divorce' as these problems are officially defined or interpreted may turn out to be misleading or naive. Whatever problem or topic is selected for investigation by sociologists there are a number of ways it can be approached. There is, for example, no single infallible approach to the study of illness and its social aspects. How it is understood and explained depends on the questions asked about it and the methods used to investigate it. Similarly there is a variety of sociological approaches used in studying the topics to which I have referred here and in the course of the book.

To summarise the arguments put forward here, information from sociological research and various sociological theories may be used in social work practice because social workers need to take cognizance of social structures and processes of change in groups and individuals. Contemporary society is becoming more complex and varied and social workers can play a part in increasing understanding and co-operation among a plurality of groups. The underlying principle is an idealistic one: it is that social conflicts and social problems can be helped through rational persuasion and without violence.

Understanding and action

Before I review different sociological approaches and methods, I want to examine the assumption that understanding and acting, theorising and practising, are sharply distinct activities. In doing this I will be drawing on arguments and concepts which we will study again later.

Some researchers into social work say that there is little evidence that social workers use theory explicitly and some social scientists regard social work as theory-less practice. Others, like Hardiker and Barker (1981) and their colleagues, think it possible to work towards understanding the use of theoretical knowledge. Although some social workers say that theory should not 'intrude' into their work with clients, their hunches, prejudices and value judgements all influence their work. They are really using implicit theory rather than explicit ideas in making decisions. Knowledge becomes internalised with experience so that what seems explicit theory to an observer may be implicit to the practitioner.

Actions imply certain kinds of understanding and social workers should be clear about assumptions that underlie what they do. The 'facts' about social situations require analysis and interpretation. 'Facts' can themselves be problematic as they are often constructed and interpreted differently by different people. These processes of construction and interpretation need to be questioned and understood. Some people are more successful than others in having their version of the 'facts' accepted. Hardiker (1981) suggests that the links between conceptual frameworks and practice are rarely direct. In her work social workers' knowledge was not reducible to specific frameworks because they were invariably led to other concepts: psycho-dynamically orientated workers thought about social networks, and workers guided by unitary frameworks also considered unconscious needs and motivations. No theory currently used in social work is equally appropriate for every psycho-social problem, method of work or client group. Specialised knowledge is required because of the range of problems and the services needed to meet them.

Social theorising in everyday life is inevitable in that everyone has value systems or ideologies and makes choices and decisions in some ways related to them. Sociological theory is of central importance as the vehicle of self-consciousness about this inevitable theorising – making the implicit explicit.

We are all theorists in the sense that we are involved in making choices and decisions, in analysing, generalising and predicting. We are also all involved in social action. Although theory and practice are differentiated their connection with one another is recognised: theory must have an object. Theory and practice are processes in a real world made up of material objects and ideas. The constraints of the environment are too great to postpone action until theoretical certainty is achieved. It is perhaps worth noting that the arrogance and spurious expertise of some armchair theorists is often revealed by their ignorance of the provisional and conditional nature of theorising. The scepticism induced by the study of sociology may help social workers to face the uncertainty which characterises theory and practice. Attempts to reduce or eliminate the anxiety this arouses are seen in developments which seek to promote a narrow technical view of individuals and social work tasks. Theorising may be subordinated to particular views of practice and to the needs perceived by some for managerial and organisational control.

The relationship between knowledge and action is limited by their institutional contexts. The growth of professions and bureaucracies has profoundly affected disciplines and practices. Institutions and organisations have developed in ways of which seem to forbid pluralism, heterogeneity and cooperation in a discipline, but seem instead to foster conflict and competitiveness. Some social work teachers have expressed concern that the narrow organisational requirements of social services departments are likely to be imposed on training courses. They question the assumption that the form and content of social work must be defined by the organisational needs of statutory agencies, and argue that this will be an anti-educational orientation. They find it understandable that social work education is seen by some managers of social work agencies as an impediment to their control of social work practice, and underline the distinction between social work education and a form of apprentice training. These social work teachers see social work education as encouraging social workers to be critical of the environments, including the agencies, in which they work, and also as helping them to build up their confidence so that they become better able to act autonomously. They also see it as helping social workers to respond sensitively and in the light of the needs of particular people and situations to what they actually meet in practice. This is a view of education for social work which is not aimed at producing compliant technicians who will uncritically implement agency policies and procedures laid down by senior staff so that they can know how a social worker will behave in this or that situation (Ackhurst, 1980). Obviously theory has to have regard for practice, but practical pressures cannot be permitted to have an overwhelming influence.

We can categorise the knowledge available to social workers as explanatory and intervention knowledge. They are not mutually exclusive. Explanatory theories and knowledge help social workers in assessing situations and problems, and sociology can make a significant contribution here. Intervention theories and knowledge help social workers to decide what to do when they have made their assessments. Ideally assessments involve integration of knowledge and practice experience, and systematically exploring the principles of change and procedures for implementing them (Fischer, 1971). I think it is important to recognise that the relationship between theory and practice is reciprocal. Applying knowledge is a tool for assessing its usefulness. Knowledge informs and influences intervention and in retrospect helps assess why intervention was or was not successful. This increment to knowledge helps identify gaps and weaknesses in the existing knowledge base. The ways in which social workers understand or interpret human behaviour in a social context are focused and shaped by basic concepts from psychology, economics and sociology. Using a variety of these ideas they may attempt to identify those which are particularly useful for practice.

Psychological ideas about personal growth and change are enhanced through analysis of socio-cultural influences on behaviour. Insight into differential access to resources that strengthen or reduce the ability of individuals to cope with change gives a broader view of possibilities of intervention. To be useful to social workers a theoretical model needs to be descriptive, accurately presenting the reality it seeks to explain, and prescriptive, providing a basis for efforts towards change. The systems approach is an example of this kind of model. It provides a convenient frame of reference to make sense of a considerable amount of information from a variety of sources, and deals with it at different levels. If a model accurately reflects the reality it attempts to describe, it is potentially of benefit social workers. Systems thinking is a way of organising information about human behaviour and the social environment with the aim of providing better understanding of intervention. It is a way of thinking which is contextual and interactional. This means that the social worker tries to understand behaviour in terms of the social context in which it occurs. Interactional analysis suggests that the social worker is concerned with interactions between people and the human and non-human systems that make up their environments.

Sociology, then, can be thought of as having certain distinct but related approaches which overlap with one another. It is a matter of debate how these different approaches are defined and the analysis in the next section should therefore be regarded as provisional and tentative. It needs to be remembered that sociologists are not the only people who are interested in social relationships. Economists and lawyers, for example, are concerned with social processes, but a moment's reflection shows that their areas of interest are different. The major concerns of sociology are the study of social structure, life styles in society and social 'problems' such as racial and class tensions, delinquency, mental disorder and poverty, and conflict and change in communities.

The term 'social structure' is an important one, though it is difficult to define. It refers to the recurring patterns of social life although how this patterning occurs is controversial. The idea is that society is differentiated and it is the social structure which 'explains' the economic base of the class system and the exploitation of one social group by another. Members of society usually take their culture for granted. The culture of a society is the way of life of its members; it largely determines how they think and feel and thus influences their actions. Since the accepted ways of behaving vary from society to society there can be considerable misunderstanding between members of different societies. Sociologists are interested in cultural differences and in uncovering the basis of social practices although it seems that this is a task which can never be finalised; it is not possible to rest for long with any particular version of 'reality' since theory and reality constantly change and human knowledge is fallible and limited.

Functionalist approaches

Functionalist approaches see society as a system the parts of which are interrelated and form an integrated whole. These parts of the system, social institutions, are analysed in terms of their functions, and how they enable society to survive. Functions are defined as those consequences of any social activity which make for the adaptation of the parts of the system. The social system is made up of people who have positions and roles. Functionalists have seen people as acting according to established norms or rules. The person thus seems to be determined by social constraints or norms. According to this view there is little room for creativity and choice, and it led to the criticism that sociology has an over-social conception of man (Wrong, 1961). Functionalist theory assumes that a certain degree of order and stability are essential for the survival of social systems. It is concerned with explaining the origin and maintenance of order and stability in society. Shared values are often seen as the key to this explanation: value consensus integrates the various parts of society. It forms the basis of social unity or social solidarity, as individuals tend to identify with those whose values they share. Many functionalists are concerned with how consensus is maintained so that emphasis is placed on the process of socialisation by which values are internalised and trans-mitted: the family is regarded as a vital part of the social structure. For functionalists integration is a necessity for the survival of communities. Whether the system is the state, a trade union or a club, it must try to keep conflict between its parts at a minimum. Disharmony must be kept in check in the interests of the effective functioning of the system. Social control functions are unavoidable, and welfare provision may be seen as contributing to its maintenance.

Secondly, a community or other group needs to have some sentiments of solidarity. Altruistic institutions and practices express concern for members of the community or group, and they tend to be normal features of society. In this approach social problems are just aberrations produced by accidents of birth or malfunctioning of social institutions like the family and the school that are responsible for transmitting social values and norms. From this point of view social problems can be solved by rehabilitating or punishing deviants, or by correcting institutional imperfections. They have little to do with central social values or social structure. Their concep-tualisation of the socialisation process provides functionalists with a theoretical framework for 'explaining' deviance. Deviants are seen as those who have been inadequately socialised and who are not sufficiently committed to the norms of their society. This assumption about the nature of deviance leads functionalists to investigate early childhood experiences, as it is in the family that basic socialisation is carried out. Deviance is defined in terms of the dominant value system, and is seen as a pathological state. At the macro level it can be interpreted as a disturbance of the equilibrium of the social system which requires the intervention of agents of social control.

Sociology and psycho-analysis

The view of human nature implicit in functionalist approaches was based on the assumption that man was a role player constantly seeking social approval and status, and that people conformed to others' expectations whether they were peers, inferiors or superiors. According to Wrong (1961), Freud's theory of human nature was more satisfactory as he did not hold that instincts directly caused behaviour uninfluenced by the surrounding cultural values. To Freud, man's social nature is the source of conflicts and antagonisms that create resistance to socialisation. Wrong pointed out that although Parsons tried to integrate Freud's theory of personality development into his framework, he underestimated the importance of conflict within the individual and between the individual and his culture and society. Before he was influenced by psycho-analytic theory, Parsons took the view that social norms are constitutive rather than merely regulative of human nature and he did not substantially alter this view. As a result, he lost the stress Freud placed on conflict. We are aware of the important influence psycho-analytic concepts have had on the development of social work as well as on practice today. Although many social workers today react against what is sometimes regarded as the confined 'psychologism' of psycho-analysis, it continues to be an important influence on social work with individuals and families. It is an approach which cannot be lightly dismissed, and is often incorporated in the ideas of many practitioners and included in social work education, usually in learning about human growth and development. This heightens interest in the way the subject is approached by sociologists and how they employ its insights. Some features of psycho-analysis may not be wholly acceptable to sociologists. We have seen that it may not be entirely congenial to some sociologists committed to functionalist, Marxist or interactionist approaches. It may be used by any of these people however, and attempts have been made to combine Marxist and Freudian approaches. There are difficulties also in reconciling aspects of psycho-analysis and some interactionist approaches, which may regard notions of unconscious motives as suspect.

Various groups of writers have used Freud's ideas in sociology, and some sociology courses now include the study of psycho-analytic theory. When this is not included it is frequently because Freud is seen as being primarily concerned with the individual, and because his social theory is seen as intellectually weak. There have always been some sociologists who see his work as not being confined to individuals. For example, the concept of the super-ego links with sociological views of the way in which values are learned and internalised in the course of socialisation. Sociologists committed to Marxist approaches are concerned with issues of conflict, and find it easier to assimilate Freudian theory than systems theorists do. Freud's concepts and theories are crucial for sociological thought, and his work is important for sociology because of the models of society and social relationships which he developed. We find that Freud's ideas about socialisation and the family led to research in this field by sociologists like Talcott Parsons, and social psychologists like Erikson, for example. Freud's theories about the relationship between sexuality and culture have been incorporated in radical sociological theories of ideological domination and extended debates about gender and sex roles. His theories constitute a necessary corrective to theories which seek to explain all social action in terms of external processes essentially determined by economic forces. In these theories questions about the rationality or non-rationality of individuals become subordinated to the logic of systems. They suffer from lack of adequate description of individual action and behaviour. Freud's ideas have been extensively used to supply models of personality development which are more adequate accounts of social action at the level of small-scale interaction.

Marxist and critical approaches

With the decline of functionalism during the 1970s, Marxist and critical theories became more influential, and were seen as offering radical alternatives to the earlier dominant theory. There are various interpretations of the work of Marx, but everyone sees society as an inter-related system of parts with the economy as the principal influence on the others. For Marxists the key to social change, which can be studied systematically, lies in relationships in the economic order. The need to subsist exists in all societies, and how subsistence is achieved has a critical effect on the whole social structure. Marx did not produce a theory of social stratification: he was not interested in describing the class system in itself, but sought to discover the principles of social change. He tried to identify those key groups which seemed to have an interest in maintaining the existing social system and those which sought to change it. Social change came about through the economic, legal, political and possibly military struggle between these two groups.

Sociologists influenced by the critical philosophy of the Frankfurt School (for example, Adorno, Fromm, Habermas and Marcuse) use a phenomenological approach and stress the creative and re-creative capacities of people and their ability to intervene and change the course of social life. They have critically analysed the capitalist system and have been concerned with many topics, including the structures of organisations and personality development. Critical analysis, particularly associated with Marcuse, was influential in the growth of liberation movements of the 1960s. It was hoped that responsibility for the nature of society and refusal to conform to role expectations and submission to the demands of large organisations would lead to simpler, more humane ways of living. Continuing critical analyses have concerned the apparent powerlessness of people in the grip of large organisations which they seem unable to control. The sense of powerlessness makes for apathy and acceptance of the status quo; humanistic psychologists like Rogers and Maslow commented on the sub-culture of despair. Critical theorists are concerned about the fragmentation which is the basis on which the social sciences are built. The distinction of subject from object, of being from consciousness, of the self from the social, of reason from feeling, are essential taken-for-granted tools of scientific thought. The thought world of sociology is deeply dualistic, a universe of social actors and social facts, of meaning and structure, observer and observed. Such observations led to the conclusion that contemporary social science analyses peoples' behaviour but fails to understand their experience.

Interactionist approaches

Interactionism covers a number of related perspectives which seek to understand the process of action between individuals. Interactionism differs from functionalism and Marxism because: (i) it focuses on small-scale interaction rather than society as a whole; (ii) usually the notion of a social system is rejected; and (iii) it does not regard human action simply as a response or reaction to the system. Interactionism has been described as a phenomenological perspective because of its emphasis on the actors' views and interpretations of social reality. It is concerned with the 'inner' or phenomenological aspects of human behaviour. From a phenomenological viewpoint the social world is a world of meaning. There is no objective reality which lies behind that meaning: the social world is not composed of entities which are external to the subjective experience of its members. To treat its aspects as 'social facts' or 'things' is to misrepresent social reality. The approach can be illustrated by reference to work on suicide and crime. Interactionists start from the assumption that action is meaningful to those involved, so that an understanding of action requires an interpretation of the meaning which actors give to their activities. Meanings are not fixed, but partly depend on the context of interaction; they are also created, developed, modified and changed in the actual process of interaction. Actions depend in part of the actors' interpretations of the ways others see them. For this reason many interactionists emphasise the idea of the self. They say that the individual develops a self-concept, a picture of self, which influences actions. A self-concept develops from interaction processes since it is largely a reflection of the actions of others towards the individual: actors tend to act in terms of their self-concepts. If people are consistently defined as disreputable or respectable, servile or arrogant, they will tend to see themselves in this way and act accordingly.

Methods of investigation in sociology

Both social workers and sociologists attempt to understand peoples' situations and how they perceive them and how they set about trying to change them or resist attempts to introduce change. Each group finds interviewing methods of interest, and it is worth bearing in mind the important place of questions in many kinds of interviews. In sociology, as in social work, methods of investigation are supposed to be decided by what is being studied. Different methods are favoured by different schools of thought, and it is misleading to assume that any one method is always appropriate and that other methods, conversely, are unhelpful or useless. There are some parallels between the methods of investigation used by sociologists and information gathering by social workers. Both groups can learn from one another as well as from other disciplines about obstacles to interpersonal communication and possible ways to modify them.

We have seen that what I have termed interactionist approaches are not likely to claim allegiance to the methods and assumptions of the natural sciences. Their concern is with actors' views and interpretations of social reality and how they attach meaning to everyday existence. This group of approaches repays study by social workers. Interactionist approaches to the social work interview have been described by Fitzjohn (1974), and she discussed the ways that clients and social workers perceive each other's roles. Interactionists' methods are not based on questionnaires and tightly structured interviews, but are aimed at greater informality and at meeting people on their own territory rather than under special or controlled conditions. They seek to observe things as they happen, and to build up confidence with the individuals and groups they are studying. Interviews are likely to be unstructured, and subjects are encouraged to expand at length in their own way about their experiences. Tape recorders are often used so that there is an accurate record of what is said. There is no claim to objectivity in the positivist sense, because sociologists using these informal methods recognise that their participation in discussion and their observations of the action in some sense changes it as they in turn are changed by it. If their conclusions are to be credible they must ensure that their analysis is rigorous and consistent. They have to identify the subjective meanings which influence the behaviour of the people they are studying, and to try to see things from their point of view. They then have to analyse and interpret what people say and what they do, and try to find the reasons for their behaviour.

Surveys and questionnaires are well-known positivist methods. They provide for large numbers of people to be questioned either by leaving a questionnaire to be returned after they have completed it, or in person. Sometimes the method is used with smaller numbers. Questionnaires may be completed by the investigator in person. This will influence respondents in various ways. For example, some people may give replies which they think the interviewer wants to hear or will approve of, rather than what they believe. But this is usually regarded as the most reliable way of getting questionnaires completed. It is not easy to produce questions which are straightforward and simply-worded and phrased as unambiguously as possible. When drawing up schedules it is easy for researchers to overlook how circumscribed their own experience is, and to take for granted that whatever a word means to them it will mean to everyone else. Another problem is loaded questions – those worded so that they are not neutral. They suggest what the answer should be or indicate the questioner's own point of view. Leading questions or statements may be made inadvertently because an interviewer does not state alternatives. This often happens because alternatives are only implied or simply regarded as obvious, and thus taken for granted. A question becomes less leading when alternatives are stated explicitly to the respondent. 'How much trouble have your neighbours been to you?' fails to suggest a negative alternative, but the effect can be modified without changing the wording by following it with:

1. 'a lot of trouble'
2. 'some trouble'
3. 'little trouble'
4. 'no trouble'

The wording or word order is still loaded, but the four alternatives answers do make a negative answer acceptable. Deliberately leading questions have a place, for example, in studying socially disapproved activities and attitudes. Questions in the form 'when did you last beat your wife?' put the onus of clarifying the activity on respondents and make them feel that wife beating is not unknown.

Many questions are loaded with associations with status or prestige. There is no simple answer to the problem that respondents make exaggerated claims about their capacity as consumers, their personal cleanliness, or their supposed prestigious taste in cars or clothes! Questions about income, occupation, education and age, for example, are very open to prestige bias. It needs to be borne in mind, though, that people do not just exaggerate or make high claims: they often understate, an example being how many cigarettes smokers say they consume. Sociologists note that people do not like to admit to foolish or reprehensible behaviour, and are usually averse to admitting to being ignorant. They are reluctant to admit to being on unfamiliar ground sometimes, or not understanding a question. But these possibilities have to be borne in mind by investigators who should not assume that everyone will be knowledgeable or have an opinion about any given topic. As this discussion reminds us, there are several reasons why a question can be embarrassing. It may be about socially disapproved behaviour such as tobacco and alcohol consumption, or law breaking. Parents being asked about their children pilfering find it easier if they are offered alternative responses such as:

1. 'Never takes anything that belongs to someone else.'
2. 'Has helped himself to someone else's things at least once or twice (including taking things belonging to other members of the family).'
3. Has stolen things on several occasions.' Using categories like these in a questionnaire and guaranteeing anonymity has been found helpful in dealing with these problems.

Although what has been said may seem trite or obvious when it is set down in writing, it illustrates the concern shared by sociologists, social workers and many others, about barriers to communication and ways to deal with them. An interview, of course, may not consist only of questions and answers, but this is an easy way in which to think of conventional exchanges. Sometimes comments replace questions but have a similar place in conversations so that similar considerations may apply to them. For the purpose of framing practical suggestions for interviewing, closed and open comments and questions can be distinguished. Closed questions are sufficient when the client is able to provide adequate information, and is able to state his or her ideas about the subject of the interview clearly and in ways the social worker readily understands. Closed questions are often sufficient when the social worker is already well informed about the client and when there are no major barriers to communication. Closed questions are appropriate when a social worker is seeking information for the purpose of categorising a request or presenting-problem, classifying, needs or establishing whether someone is eligible to receive certain services. Certain key questions, for example, are helpful in assessing whether a person is eligible for registration as being disabled, or whether they should apply for certain social security benefits. The social worker may need to ask follow-up questions and to probe further to obtain supplementary information. This may lead to discussion of other topics or related problems.

Open questions are used when the purpose of an interviewer is not restricted to categorising an application or problem, but is concerned with less clear-cut topics such as a person's attitudes or feelings or family relationships. Social workers use open questions when they have little information about clients, and when clients need to think through ideas and problems during the interview. When social workers are not well acquainted with clients, and when there seem to be barriers to communication like the ones I describe here, they will be likely to use open-ended questions and comments and will use these to try to encourage clients to talk as freely as seems necessary. As sociologists, social workers and others gain experience, they develop greater awareness that finding out about feelings, opinions or behaviour involves framing questions in such a way as to encourage people to reply at length. They have greater understanding of the difficulty of putting people at their ease and encouraging them to talk frankly.

Conclusion

The analysis of the social framework can be made in relation to social and individual problems and in terms of elements like power, social differences, norms, positions and roles. Examining the structure facilitates analysis of patterns of the experience and behaviour of groups and individuals. It has been noted that social behaviour becomes patterned and orderly. People are not treated equally by the social system. Criteria like sex, age, race and social class are used to differentiate between them. A considerable amount of information about social differentiation and stratification processes is available. Although relationships between social stratification processes, access to resources and power are perceived, theories to 'make sense' of the information are elusive. But through the process of assigning people to different positions and roles differences are created which have fundamental effects on peoples' lives. Personality is seen in the roles people play and unemployment shows the dangers to personality when roles are lost. We have studied the objective view of the social system as a framework of groups and institutions and the underlying ideas and values. People living in it perceive and experience the social system subjectively and individuals take account of the elements of the social structure in making choices and decisions; in a sense you could say that everyone is a social theorist. A theoretical model needs to present accurately the reality it seeks to explain and to provide a basis for efforts towards change. The systems approach has been said to provide a frame of reference to make sense of information from various sources. Different sociological perspectives have been discussed and the value of psycho-analytic ideas has been examined. Some of these topics are developed in the next chapter.

We have seen that one view of social work is as that of a bridge between the 'deviant' and 'society'. This suggests that it is hoped that the deviant individual can be 'rehabilitated' back into society. This assumes that he or she can come to accept the values and norms of wider society. Although it may be rare for people to relinquish their commitment to all commonly-held values, when this does occur many social workers might feel they have little to offer. But one reason for stressing the uncertainties of social work is to suggest the need for social workers to persevere in such situations. In the first place it is not at all easy to assess how far an individual has withdrawn from social life and has rejected group norms. Second, the present state of knowledge does not (or should not) permit us to 'write people off' in a summary way. Third, different perspectives on problems sometimes suggest new approaches in dealing with them. This may be illustrated briefly by discussing the general notion of deviance. Some theories define deviance as the breaking of some commonly-accepted rules and seek the causes of the rule breaking in the social situations of deviants. Theories about delinquency, for example, have been related to ideas about the status frustrations of working-class adolescents. For some, the desire for achievement, excitement and status cannot be met in traditional ways in pubs or working-men's clubs. The unsuccessful search for excitement may include riding bikes and meeting in cafés and discos. When these become boring, delinquency and rowdyism may replace them. A delinquent sub-culture may thus provide an outlet for some dissatisfactions. Other theories take the reaction to so-called deviant acts as their starting point. This contrasts with those approaches which saw deviance as a quality of rule breaking and which took official definitions of acts as deviant as their starting point. To interactionists, however, deviance is seen as a consequence of the application by others of rules and sanctions to an offender. There is thus less interest in the personal and social characteristics of deviants and more interest in the process by which some people come to be labelled as outsiders and their reactions to this process.

In subsequent chapters I shall refer to social problems and how these can be studied on different social levels, from the individual to the macro-social. These different ways of looking at social problems are sometimes in conflict with one another but they are sometimes complementary. We need to bear this in mind because different perspectives have implications for the nature and scale of preventive and interventive measures. It can hardly be expected that we shall deal with a great number of social problems and different views on them in the limited space of this book. Readers should therefore study these topics as illustrations of ideas which have wider applications.

2
Sociology and Social Problems

This chapter deals with some contributions made by sociologists to the study of social problems. Ideas about norms and power are central to sociological approaches to defining and describing social problems and their analysis raises complex issues. Approaches to the study of the family and family problems, mental illness, unemployment and social policy provide further illustrations and indicate the controversial nature of the relationships between sociology, social policy and social work. Analysis of these issues forms a basis for later discussion of practice. There are some problems which are not 'social' in the sense that the answers do not depend on the nature of the society in which an individual lives. Being handicapped by paralysis or blindness gives rise to problems in social life, but there can be no social measures which can adequately resolve them. Questions like 'why am I blind (or paralysed)?' or 'how am I to cope with my handicap?' illustrate this: social measures can only alleviate the conditions. Peoples' attitudes on their own deaths and the deaths of others, how they orientate themselves to anticipating and experiencing death, are human problems or existential problems. It has been suggested that a social problem exists when: (i) there is a conflict between sizeable segments of the population; (ii) the conflict is seen in direct confrontation between opposing groups; (iii) the conflict is expressed in terms of moral issues – for example, of justice and injustice, right and wrong; (iv) the conflict is accompanied by efforts to change significant social institutions and the rules governing the relations between individuals and groups; (v) when there

23

is a degree of challenge to political authority; and (vi) strong emotions are produced by the conflict over moral issues (Tallman, 1976).

Unemployment, mental illness and sociology

There is nothing inherent in the sociologists' attempt to understand society that necessarily leads to the practice of social work, although a grasp of sociology is of great use to the social worker as well as to nurses, doctors and politicians. Sociological understanding has served to uncover unsatisfactorily social conditions, and has cleared away collective illusions about social problems such as poverty, and issues in such areas as penal practice, racial harmony, education and urban living. It has to be recognised that sociological understanding can be applied with opposite intentions. Understanding of racial prejudice can be applied as effectively by those fomenting hatred as by those seeking to increase tolerance. The social problem of mental disorder is largely a problem of dealing with individual patients. The problem may be discussed in more general terms in political debate, but the everyday problems of the health and social services are how to deal with particular individuals. The 'solutions' are obviously affected by considerations of economic and political expedience, moral beliefs and often unspoken taken-for-granted assumptions about ways of dealing with psychiatric casualties.

To illustrate sociological approaches to social problems we can look at how they contribute to understanding of mental illness. One way is to look at social factors involved in the process by which people are labelled as mentally ill and at what happens to them subsequently. Most of the available evidence seems to support the view that applying a label of mental illness in some instances has more or less serious negative consequences for a number of people. It seems that once some people are labelled, the reactions of others towards them and their own self-perceptions will be more or less permanently changed. They become identified primarily with a deviant role, in their case that of the mentally ill. This identity overrides most of the other identities they have had and becomes a sort of master status. Such changes are difficult to assess directly. It has been shown that people who behaved in ways usually taken to indicate mental illness were rejected by others, and a direct correlation has been found between the severity of disturbance attributed to a particular person and the likelihood that he would be rejected. But it is the appearance of psychological symptoms rather than the knowledge that someone has been labelled as mentally ill which conditions people's responses. Labelling will only be effective in the sense of persuading the labelee to accept the label, if the label is consistent with the person's own prior self-conception, and if the label fits a general category that the person is predisposed to accept (Rotenburg, 1975). Such findings suggest that ways can be found to either reduce or reverse the impact of labelling even in the area of mental illness.

Another way sociology contributes to understanding is by considering mental illness as a social construct and examining how it is defined by those involved and how both patients and would-be helpers act. For people to be enabled to avoid mental illness it appears that they need to achieve happiness and a degree of satisfaction in key roles in society, as children in families and at school, as adults, as employees deriving satisfaction from work and as members of families, as parents or partners, for example. Serious problems may arise from failure in any of these roles, and this is likely to lead to tension, stress and instability. While some people seem to be able to cope by finding that success in one area of life compensates for unhappiness in another, for many breakdown of a key role will lead to mental illness and the subsequent career of a patient. There is a need for flexibility and mobility of many groups of workers because of changes in the economic structure. Thus risks are involved in 'spiralist' professions (such as medicine, teaching and some industrial posts) where a high degree of geographical mobility is required. Families may not be in one area long enough to put down roots, and relationships with distant friends and relatives may suffer. When 'spiralists' come from working-class backgrounds where family ties are close, the difficulties are increased as acceptance of the career ethos may involve rejecting family norms. Children's school careers may suffer because of their parents' employment. The stress involved in demanding jobs like coal mining and fishing has been studied, and the arduous and dangerous nature of this work are among obvious threats to mental well-being. Other threats to which sociologists have given attention are those found in boring repetitive work: the effects of tedious work overflow into other areas of living and produce neurotic symptoms. There are also occupations where people's work ideologies conflict with those of wider society, crime being one example. Prostitutes elicit conflicting attitudes in that they are often publicly condemned, but their services are greatly enjoyed and approved in private. Ministers of religion face stress in trying to work in agnostic societies. Other occupations whose ethos may conflict with wider society are those of advertising and selling goods like cigarettes and drugs, which are not universally approved. The salesman faces many stresses with the constant need to maintain sales and to travel, so that family life is disrupted. Unemployment can contribute to mental illness. The ex-worker may have dependents to support, and may feel stigmatised with the loss of the central occupational role. Women face mental health problems in both deciding and attempting to return to work after they have children.

It is likely that young people leaving school and finding no jobs available will experience feelings of uselessness and frustration, and may be drawn into delinquency. People already disadvantaged in the acquisition of work skills are most prone to unemployment. Unemployment deprives people of the company of workmates, of activities and interests, of income, a sense of purpose and of a source of personal identity and self-esteem. It produces changes in the assumptions people make about themselves and in their ways of relating to others. The assumptions they make about their identity as individuals are put under pressure. Adjustment to this situation and other situations involving loss or depriva-tion involves trying to re-establish a good 'fit' between the individual and the environment. Where a change is experi-enced as a loss, letting go of old assumptions and identities can be difficult and sometimes painful. Interactionist approaches use various concepts to help understand how individuals may try to cope with and manage some aspects of their social environments. People without work may feel that they have to try to stage 'manage' their interactions with others. They may nevertheless fail to defend themselves against unacceptable definitions which others may try to impose on them, and it may involve complicated manoeuvres to counter unacceptable definitions. For example, unemployed people sometimes make the sort of statements that they feel others may make against them because they are not at work. A man may joke about being aware that he is living on other people's taxes. By bringing this out into the open he is not denigrating himself but is preventing others from using it to criticise him, and by joking about it he shows that he does not regard it as serious criticism. By showing others that they will not hurt him he also shows them that it is not worth their trying to do so. This is in some ways like the situation of the former psychiatric hospital patient. When she leaves hospital she finds that she is now categorised as someone who is regarded as socially incompetent, unpredictable and undesirable, and may try to change this situation by changing the classification of herself. One way of doing this is to assert that the hospital admission was a 'mistake', and that she should have gone to a different kind of hospital. Her aim is thus to show that in the past she was not socially incompetent and undesirable, and therefore is not like that now. She does not conceal the fact of illness, but tries to disguise its nature and minimise its social consequences. An alternative response is to tell people about the experience of mental illness and to hide nothing. Some ex-patients decide to explain the nature of their problems and how to overcome them, while others demonstrate that they have changed in positive ways.

Mental illness and hospitalisation affect occupational careers. Former psychiatric patients experience difficulties in obtaining and retaining employment, and even the knowledge of previous mental illness can hinder occupational advance. In industrial society economic and material advances should mean that people are protected against hunger and material need, but it seems that this can only be achieved at the cost of loneliness and alienaton. It seems that people rely for meaning and dignity in their lives on a few relationships, and when these fail mental illness may often occur. I will be referring to the social problems of loneliness and alienation, and social work practice in the course of this book. I will also be discussing the role of social factors in mental disorder and its treatment. Their importance is seen in a recent study of the social networks of schizophrenic patients which indicated that the structural as well as the interpersonal characteristics of these networks needed to be taken into account. Taylor, Huxley and Johnson (1984) examined the hypothesis that the level of social support available to the closest associate of the schizophrenic patient is linked to the level of functioning found in the patient. They were unable to draw any firm conclusions about how the relative's social network is implicated in the patient's condition. But they suggested that on the one hand the comparative social isolation of a relative may act to reduce his own expectations of a patient, while on the other, it could be that relatives of patients with poor social performance are those showing the highest levels of encouragement to the patient. Living with a patient who has a poor level of adjustment may make it difficult for the relative to maintain a normal pattern of social interaction, particularly with non-kin and with people in varied and unconnected settings.

Perspectives on the family

Much sociological research on the family has been within the functionalist tradition. The underlying assumption of this approach is that the family is fundamental to most, if not all, societies, and everything should be done to preserve it. The possibility that the various functions of the family could be organised in different structures is excluded. It is assumed that a number of dysfunctions of the family can be identified and 'managed' in some way: this illustrates the conservative assumptions of functionalist theory.

In line with the interest in the contribution made by social institutions to the working of society, the family is said to perform functions which include:

1. The organisation of sexual behaviour.
2. The physical care of children.
3. The socialisation of children, as well as other family members, to have values and to behave in ways expected by society.
4. The division of labour between husband and wife.
5. The definition of roles in the family such as wife and mother, husband and father, son and daughter, which enable people to learn what is expected of them and what they may expect of others.
6. Provision for the physical and psychological support of family members in a loving, intimate groups which often contrasts with an alien and impersonal society.

From the functionalist point of view 'normal' family life is a stable, secure, happy and lasting arrangement. When it is functioning properly the family unit provides for the rearing of children and for the basic needs of all its members. On this view roles are appropriately defined and work is divided in the family in ways which best fit in with the economic and social system. This kind of picture is not popular now because it begs many important questions about family life. Many people experience family life very differently. The family for them is a source of unhappiness and conflict, and many families are split by marital disharmony, divorce and violence. Another problem is that the functionalist view is founded on unexamined values and assumptions. In defining certain kinds of behaviour as normal the way is open to 'medicalise' marriage, and provide therapy for the family, trends associated with systems theorising (Morgan, 1985).

Phenomenological and symbolic interactionist studies have provided interesting new insights into the family, the identities and self-images of family members and family behaviour. These are all seen as socially constructed realities, and the way these realities are built up, maintained and changed over time and the consequences for individual behaviour, have been studied. What the family means to its members and others, how fuzzy or how solid its boundaries are, and how it is changed in the course of time, are all related to interaction in the family. The mechanisms or resources used in the process of reality construction include:

1. Major events and crises that go to make up family themes such as the chronic illness of a member, using a mentally handicapped child as a scapegoat, or the labelling of someone as being difficult or awkward, or a set of shared experiences.
2. The use of ritual in family living, such as those rituals associated with the life cycle of individuals, or the family unit, or idiosyncratic rituals like mother bringing home gifts for father and child on Friday night, or elaborations of daily routines.
3. The use of the home and space within it, seen, for example, in the reservation of a special room for the entertainment of visitors when the family puts on a performance for non-family members.

Morgan (1985) argues that the phenomenological orientation is particularly relevant in the study of the family since it is here and in the study of gender that so much is taken for granted, and where many everyday assumptions are carried over into sociological models.

The Marxist approach may be seen as being committed to the notion of the family as changing and evolving. This is similar to the emphasis on processes of change which are part of Marxist understandings of classes and society generally. Ideas about the class struggle, too, have been linked to evolutionary understandings of the development of the family. One of the strengths of the Marxist perspective is that it deals with the economic dimensions of family life and not only in terms of its role in the wider economic system. The family is seen as an economic system in its own right. In traditional Marxist theory private property was seen as having a crucial role in shaping the development of the family and in underlining patriarchal authority. Furthermore, the family is seen as reproducing class inequalities and perpetuating sexual inequality and antagonism within the family and marriage. Instead of emphasising the relatively harmonious fit or adjustment between family and society the Marxist approach highlights contradictions in the relationship. Marxist commitment to change in the family seems to be very tentative, but the reasons seem to be very complex. They are discussed by Coward (1983).

Marxists argue that capitalist society is not simply maintained by dominant groups, but that socialisation creates psychological conditions in individuals so that they fit into existing social structures. Even when located in underprivileged groups, the family transmits norms promoted by the dominant class. To maintain its integrity the political system has to mobilise support continuously, or at least to keep people in a state of indifference. The family seeks to socialise the young to accept the political and economic system to which it has accommodated itself, and in this way acts as the psychological agent of society (Fromm, 1968). Modern industrial society is thought to be characterised by a split between a public sphere made up of bureaucratic institutions which regulate the individual's economic, political and cultural life, and a private sphere. The public institutions confront the individual as powerful, alien and incomprehensible, and 'society' is not experienced as the joint creation of individuals. In capitalist society individuals are dwarfed and rendered powerless in the face of institutions they cannot understand and control. Alienated from society, they attempt to find 'real life' in the private sphere of family and friends (Berger, 1966). Marriage thus assumes considerable importance as a sanctuary for retreat from the public sphere, and the family as the place where people recover a sense of human worth. Marriage is seen simply as a form of private property. In the capitalist socio-economic system people relate to virtually everything of value by individual ownership. It is also necessary to criticise idealised images of marriage where there is a failure to show the husband-wife relationship as one of power, in which women are subordinated (Scanzoni, 1972). From the Marxist standpoint no particular kind of family organisation is seen as universally suitable. A range of institutions is thought to be needed to provide for the variety of men and women. To create this situation women should be integrated into the economy, non-sexist patterns of socialisation should be established, similar educational aspirations in both sexes should be encouraged and, in the longer term, the capitalist system should be replaced by democratic socialism where production is subordinated to social welfare (Mitchell, 1975).

Developments in feminism in the 1960s and 1970s led to the family being seen as the key institution in the determination and perpetuation of the subordinate status of women. These developments were politically distinct from the earlier concentration on women's rights and opportunities outside the home. What was particularly striking about these trends was the argument that personal experiences were not isolated phenomena, but the product of social circumstances which affected women in a systematic way and the explicit challenge they posed to the existing form and ideology of the nuclear family. An important feature of feminist approaches to the family has been the inclusion of a critique of Marxism as well as orthodox sociology because women have found themselves marginalised equally in socialist and in more orthodox movements. While there are important differences between feminist and Marxist approaches, they agree that it is not enough to provide detailed theoretical analyses of capitalism and patriarchy: both systems need to be changed. The feminist movement since the late 1960s has concentrated not simply on the sociology of the family but also on the sociology of work, education, deviance and class. It has also questioned and attacked the main assumptions that have guided research and theorising. Thus some of the main assumptions underlying research and theory have been scrutinised in a radical way. Since the late 1960s, then, the feminists have, together with Marxists, engaged in a thorough critical appraisal of orthodox sociology itself, for its tendency to present bourgeois ideology as if it were social science. They have noted that the ranks of sociologists are dominated by males. Their dominance has not only served to shape research and theorising so that women are either invisible or are seen as deviating from male-defined norms. It may be that the effects have not been direct nor blatant, but it is still regarded as pervasive. The pervasive nature of male domination is legitimated all the time by being regarded as natural. Feminists have been critical of the main assumptions which have been thought to guide research and theorising, and also of the institutions in which research is carried on. Gender differentiations in the family are not seen as merely a particular case of domestic divisions but as the central division. In the feminist analysis emphasis is placed on division of resources in the household and the way the household contributes to the wider sexual division of labour. The family is analysed not simply in terms of its relationship to wider society nor in terms of its functions, but as a particular site of women's oppression (see Burman, 1979, and Randall, 1982).

The family, social policy and sociology

A compromise between the radical and traditional positions recognises: (a) that some family problems arise within the individual; (b) that some are generated by the social system; and (c) that many result from interaction between the two. Change is not resisted, and it is assumed that the family is a flexible institution which can and does adapt to social changes, and that it can be helped to adapt by policies based on knowledge of the processes involved in the creation and resolution of social problems. From the functionalist point of view the early death of the family is not anticipated, provided it continues to fulfil its functions, especially socialisation. Functionalists thought that the performance of a function creates an obligation and that society has a duty to provide the most favourable conditions in which the family can operate. They argued that in modern Britain people put a positive value on the family and support for the institution is a social value: policies have to be based on this consensus if they are to be valid in a democratic state. These ideas are basic to the reforming tradition which grew up in this country in the nineteenth and twentieth centuries. The aim has been to protect families from misfortune as far as possible and try to introduce measures to reduce inequalities through redistribution of income, by providing a comprehensive health service, and by opening up the educational system. Intervention at the structural level to deal with poverty and lack of opportunity which are still prevalent, needs to include efforts to eliminate not only poverty itself but also the feeling of being poor. At any social level the feeling of missing out is a form of deprivation. This illustrates the way that not only tangible pressures, but also many intangible ones like personality and emotional problems, can affect the overall quality of family life. Problems arise from the interaction between personality and social structure when norms and values previously taken for granted are no longer appropriate as a result of social change. A topical example is the changing allocation of roles between the sexes, so that some people feel uncertain or ambivalent about their roles.

Social policies aimed at furthering the welfare of families should therefore comprise supportive services which enable family members to perform their roles well, and they should also be aimed at facilitating the adaptation of the family to changing conditions. However, although policies seem reasonable and fair when they are first conceived, they may later be regarded as unjust and inequitable if ideologies and social ideals markedly change. An example is the way the meaning of terms like 'adequate role performance' change as values change. An associated problem is how and by whom role performance is judged as adequate or not. Ironically, new family problems may be created by family policy itself, and by the social agencies whose aim is to eradicate or modify them.

A simple view of family problems is to see them as deriving from the needs of specific groups such as older people, middle-aged parents, children, and so on. But you could be a member of any of these groups without being a social casualty or a source of anxiety to others and, of course, the majority of people in these groups do not cause concern. One characteristic of a social problem is that it occasions social and/or personal distress. Natural disasters such as war and epidemics often disrupt family life, and for some people they lead to permanent personal problems. For some people, and for society also in the long term, problems evaporate once the stressful event has passed. It is useful to distinguish between a personal problem which is specific to an individual (a subjective problem) and a social problem which has wider implications (an objective problem). Whereas being widowed is a problem which can have wider social implications – society may become involved if the widow requires financial help because of insufficient income – it is also a personal problem. The widow has to make both personal and social adjustments.

In a quickly changing society it may be difficult to identify norms and values because different groups and sub-cultures may regard the same behaviour differently. Attitudes to a wide range of behaviour vary by age, religion, social class and ethnic group. Contradictory patterns of norms exist side by side – for example, those relating to the sanctity of family life and those which place a positive value on sexual freedom. In so far as family and social problems are socially defined, it is important to understand by whom they are so defined as there is often no consensus about them. But the range of tolerated behaviour tends to narrow when a society feels under pressure: the norms relating to the family and marriage tend to be less strict in wartime when the types of behaviour seen as problematic tend to decrease. Problem behaviour is relative in that prevailing economic and social conditions influence the labels attached to behaviour.

Another way of looking at family problems is as manifestations of role conflict or role strain. In the course of a lifetime each member of a family has to change his or her roles, responsibilities and tasks many times as it is the stages of moving from one role to another that is particularly critical. The birth of a baby, the child starting at school or beginning a job or leaving home, retirement from work, or the death of a partner, all involve role strain and are potential crisis situations. Adjustment to changing roles in family life is most difficult at times when social values are blurred and role expectations are not clear-cut. In contrast, more stable societies have clearer role expectations at each new stage in the life cycle.

Another way of looking at the nature of family problems is in terms of social resources. In trying to achieve their goals, people use their resources – for example, income, physical appearance, education, love and friendships of various kinds. Individuals have different quantities and combinations of such resources available, but they all have an exchange value and represent bargaining power. The more resources to which an individual or family have access, the greater the chances of goal attainment inside and outside the family. Another source of family problems is frustration, which may occur within or outside the family. There are, of course, many frustrations within the family, such as those associated with traditional feminine roles. Working-class women may feel defeated by large families, over-crowding and poor housing, and middle-class wives may be frustrated if low income leads to their being excluded from the life-style of the group. Status dissatisfaction and status ambiguity work in various ways to foster friction in the family, as when the wife has higher class origins than her partner, or when the wife's job success threatens the husband. Damage to individuals' self-images can act as a detonator of intra-familial problems which can rebound unfavourably or disastrously on the marriage and children.

The principal variables involved in family disorganisation have been identified as disregard or misunderstanding of social norms, family attitudes to stressful situations, inadequate role performance and social interaction, and poverty, some of which – poverty particularly – have been known about for some time. Adequate income is regarded as fundamental to material and emotional security. The relative significance of different factors in the causation of family breakdown may be tentatively assessed in hypothesised, linked sequences of cause and effect. The family home and its location, important in relation to the family's economic environment, is important too in other connections. In a high deliquency area the location may be felt to inhibit family members' acceptance of the prevailing norms. Poor housing exacerbates family tensions and undermines marriages which might survive in an environment which is more favourable. There is a positive association between good health and good housing, and it is affected by income. Health also impinges on other aspects of family life in that any chronic or recurrent illness, physical or mental handicap, or loss of a family member through hospital admission or death, means that family roles need readjustment. Tension may result from readjustment or failure to readjust, and there may be conflict arising from resistance to the rearrangement of roles and changes in the authority structure. Stress may also be produced by a change in the status of the family itself as changed roles and role expectations are involved when norms are changed or lost. The socially mobile family (whether upwardly or downwardly mobile) may suffer from conflict or an anomic situation may arise. Stress can be associated not only with loss of income, but also with wealth or change in status beyond what was expected; that is, in terms of individual's social backgrounds, education and achievements, and so on. The personality structures of the partners in the nuclear family have implications for the well-being of the group. Stress may be prevented from turning into a crisis if personal relationships are good, even when material resources are not adequate. Adversity can sometimes strengthen a family: this may depend on how well the group was meeting individuals' emotional needs before the stressful events occurred. Where family members are anxious and neurotic and are performing their roles inadequately, they may not be capable of pulling themselves together because of what the situation means to them, which in part reflects their personality structure. Families who overcome stresses and deal with crises effectively tend to have adequate role performances: each individual meets the expectations of others, and they quickly adapt their roles when faced with new situations or problems.

Community care and the family

There is confusion about the meaning of community care, and the post-war policy of community care has not led to a massive transfer of resources away from residential care for groups like the elderly, the mentally disordered, and children unable to live in their own homes or not having a home. The notion of community care seems to depend on having a close-knit society in which there is mutual aid between families and individuals as a basis of care: this is not the case in contemporary society. Community care has always depended on care within families, usually provided by female relatives, and families and individuals have been urged to care for themselves and not to expect help from the state. In effect, a double equation is involved: in practice community care equals help by the family, and care by the family equals care by women. In official policy, then, there has been a moral imperative to women to provide care (Finch and Groves, 1980). Some of the anomalies and contradictions referred to here are discussed in the book edited by Walker (1984). This examines the operation of community care policies in relation to children, the elderly and the mentally handicapped. The promise of policy has been translated into actual shared care for them only to a very limited extent, and it is noted that the growth of the welfare professions and their employing organisations bears directly on the development of community care policies. It is argued that the idealised picture of the nuclear family which seems implicit in the policy of community care is unrealistic. The number of people living alone or with friends and of single-parent families has been steadily increasing. Lip-service has been paid to community care by governments, but there is no national strategy regarding the closure of outmoded institutions such as large hospitals for the mentally disordered. This leads to the question whether the policy of community care ever really meant developing supportive services so as to reverse the institutionalising of people who cannot cope without help. It leads in turn to questioning whether it is correct to say that community care facilities have failed, and whether 'community care' is attractive to politicians and policy-makers because it is ambiguous and comprehends a wide range of social measures. Was the 'failure' of the idea present from the beginning? The account so far may appear to suggest that the constraints and pressures of the social structure and social policies on the social worker and families might imply that change or amelioration are hopeless aims. Such a conclusion would be misleading, since the discussion is at a general level. What it does seem to suggest is that social services staff may need to campaign, with others, to secure policy change and clarification.

Conclusion

As Worsley (1981) points out, what constitutes a 'social problem' is itself quite problematic. When we use those words such things as poverty, sickness, delinquency and crime, or family troubles normally come to mind. But war, oversized school classes and evil governments are just as much social problems. Each person and each group defines social problems differently, and what behaviour is or is not acceptable varies over time as well. In looking at social problems sociologists collect statistical and other data about aspects of the environment as a preliminary step in trying to discover relationships between, say, income and occupational status. In attempting to identify social factors which generate personal troubles, and in showing that they are not purely personal, they do not suggest that misfortunes do not happen to persons. Their approach is not confined to external factors, but is also concerned with aspects of social relations which become part of the individual's inner world. The individual experiences the break-up of his marriage, or going to prison, or losing his job. But these are social problems in the sense that the marriage partners may have absorbed absurd romantic ideas of what marriage would be like, and the delinquent may have grown up in an area where crime was common or admired. Usually the individual shares the experience of losing his job with many others and is not an isolate. We should note that the conventional idea of social problems focuses primarily on the individual affected and not on the agencies doing the affecting. We can only fully understand private troubles, some sociologists claim, by tracing the larger malfunctioning which 'causes' the individual suffering. Their concern is not with why people become criminal or mentally ill, but is rather to understand the social definitions of social problems, and the structural problems of society of which all people may not be aware. A social problem may be seen as a significant discrepancy between social standards and social actuality. In his book on social work and mental handicap, Anderson (1982) makes the point that social workers are concerned about conflicts of norms, not just to fit individuals to norms but also to rethink those norms. He emphasises that social workers are here for the misfits, in the sense of people of whom others disapprove or just do not want to know.

The relationships between social theories, social problems and social action are complicated whichever approach is used. For example, functionalists have given less weight to questions of class relations and power than Marxist theorists who have provided critical appraisals of social institutions and policies. Functionalist theory was a powerful influence on social work until the 1960s, and it supported the tendency to regard social problems in terms of individual pathology. A new radical consciousness emerged in social work and community work, and there has been growing awareness of the control functions of welfare services in society, and social work has been associated with overtly political movements working for disadvantaged and deviant groups. Problems of racism and sexism, and the rediscovery of poverty and exploitation in the USA and Britain, and the problems of capitalist economies have all helped to undermine an approach based on ideas of equilibrium, harmony and value consensus. Although there is disagreement about how to define social problems and how they should be dealt with, sociologists now see social problems as a central focus. This is useful in suggesting possible limitations of social work intervention. It helps to curb extravagant claims about the contributions social workers might make to the alleviation of problems, but the knowledge they gain in the course of their work enables social workers to act as informed critics of local and national policies. It is to be hoped that this will further our understanding of the production of social problems in society and their distribution to individuals. One of the more valuable lessons of sociology, it has been suggested, is that social problems do not necessarily arise from conditions judged to be pathological. They may be unintended and unforeseen effects of positively valued policies, for example, of care in the community.

The controversial relationship between sociology, social policy and social work is well illustrated in relation to family groups and the promotion of 'effective' role performance. The idea of a policy of community care has not been translated widely into practice since this requires transfer of resources on a large scale, and depends on having a closely-knit society characterised by mutual aid. It was argued that families experience, problems, although these might not be recognised as such by the people involved or by wider society. Many family policies are essentially aimed at promoting effective role performances in a changing society. They may be described as: (i) casualty services to deal with crises; (ii) preventive services to mitigate or avoid stress by ensuring that families have material and emotional resources to cope with the strains of the family life cycle; and (iii) measures aimed at the improvement of the quality of life for all families and not only those at risk. Because the first two categories make urgent demands they receive more emphasis than the last. I will examine some aspects of social work practice with individuals and families later.

3

Sociology, Groups and Organisations

Groups as systems

Systems theorists say that two basic problems, allocation and integration, face all groups. Human capacities and resources, facilities for the performance of roles (including power) and rewards (prestige and approval) must be allocated. If this problem is not dealt with successfully, that is when allocation impedes co-operation, a social system may disintegrate. The problem of integration follows from the need for allocation. There must be a sufficient complementarity of roles and clusters of roles for collective and personal goals to be effectively pursued, and for conflict among individuals to be kept within bounds (Parsons and Shils, 1951). The focus on the role structure (i.e. the group as a social system) has led to interpersonal processes in groups being studied on certain distinct levels. These are behaviour, emotions, norms, group goals and group values. Behaviour is the overt action of a person in the presence of others. Emotions are the drives experienced by a person and the feelings she has about others and about what happens. Norms are ideas about what a person should do, feel or express. Goals are ideas about what a group as a collective should do. Values are ideas that describe ideal states or conditions for the group. On each level, an element or entity – i.e. an act, a feeling, an idea about what a member or the group itself should do or become – is interrelated with the other entities on the same level; in other words, each level is treated as a sub-system of the groups with its own internal dynamics:

1. On the level of behaviour, the sub-system is the interaction system, which is the organisation of overt action among persons over time.
2. On the level of emotion, the sub-system is group emotion, which is the configuration of feelings among members and of their emotional responses to events that occur.
3. On the level of norms, the sub-system is the normative system, which is the organised, and largely shared, ideas about what members should do and feel, about how these should be regulated, and about what sanctions should be applied when behaviour does not coincide with the norms.
4. On the level of goals, the sub-system is the technical system, which is the set of ideas about what the group should accomplish, and the plans about how it is to be accomplished.
5. On the level of values, the sub-system is the executive system, which consists of interpretations of what the group is, the ideas about what would be desirable for it to become, and ideas about how it might so become. (Mills, 1967)

One of the ways in which sociologists think about groups then involves analysing inter-personal relationships at these five levels. This means considering the elements on each of these levels as organised into systems or sub-systems, each with its own principles of organisation. These five systems are inter-related, since people's feelings are affected by what they and others do; their actions are affected by their ideas and rules change as people's goals change. As systems, then, groups are seen as self-directing, goal-seeking and boundary-maintaining, and as responding to their environments. This view has been extended to see groups as information-processing systems. Members observe and evaluate their actions as a group in dealing with internal and external demands. They can learn from their experience how better to achieve collective goals, and may rearrange the structure of their group. For social workers it seems to be particularly important that feedback mechanisms can help people to become aware of the characteristics of their group, and can give a group the potential for self-determination and growth.

The term 'growth' refers to the development of a number of capabilities:

1. increased intake of information from the outside environment
2. a capacity to assume increased responsibilities
3. the capacity to change their goals
4. the flexibility to change customs and rules
5. the ability to admit new members.

The group is thus seen as being a source of experience and learning. The cybernetic model thus sees the group as an information-processing system. Individual members are also seen as processing information so that the model is one of both individual and group development. The model draws attention to the information that is contained in the system and its current state, and the relationship between the system and its environment. It also takes account of the observation that individuals and groups learn and grow, and helps in the analysis of groups not just concerned with survival and immediate satisfaction but whose members are interested in new goals and fresh ideas. This is not an all-encompassing model, but usefully supplements other approaches.

Pressure and conflict in groups

People vary a great deal in their reactions to being members. Extroverted individuals may take on some roles with little difficulty; examples are the leader, subversive or counter-leader, and advocate. Introverted people may more easily take on roles such as the prophet, critic and scapegoat. People align themselves differently at different times and in different situations, and contribute to the maintenance or the ending of a group. In groups people are subject to pressures, expectations, support and reinforcement. An example is peer group pressure, which appears to lead to peer conformist behaviour. This influence continues in peoples' minds even if they are not physically present in the group. Such group pressures produce norms. If they are not observed they lead to censure, mockery, rejection and exclusion. The need to belong is a very powerful sanction, and groups can make it difficult for people to withstand pressure. They can oblige their members to behave in certain ways.

According to the conflict model, the group is characterised by endless conflicts. Change is determined in both direction and quality by the way conflicts are dealt with. The group has enough resources to meet all the internal needs and to respond to all external demands. To become organised, a group has to co-ordinate members' activities, and in doing so must limit the freedom of some of its members. There is thus an inevitable conflict between individual freedom and demands on members for conformity and co-ordination. Groups accept and reward some members more fully than others, and this inequality also creates conflict. Though one conflict may be dealt with, its modification will give rise to new strains. No group is free of conflict, and a group which seems to be free of strain may not be facing up to its problems. As with individuals, groups are thought to deny, cover up and project on to others their internal conflicts, especially when they are uncertain about how to cope with them. One value of this model is to focus attention on the conflicts, hostilities and dissatisfactions which may affect a group, and it counters the assumpton that change occurs smoothly and naturally. The use of the conflict model tends to obscure the ways in which group cohesiveness comes about. It seems to overlook the possibility of mutual respect in hierarchies, and of building trust and friendship. There is also the danger that the importance of achieving consensus in promoting change is not recognised. In applying the model there is the danger of assuming that existing conflicts are of the greatest concern to sociologists and also to group members. A group leader can easily be diverted into giving more attention to keeping the peace instead of dealing with other important tasks.

Roles and norms

Each kind of group has a characteristic set of roles available to it. The roles of instrumental (or task) leader and expressive (social-emotional) leader may well occur in every kind of group, and the role of 'leader of the opposition' is often found in training groups, work groups and juries. These roles appear for a variety of reasons. There are jobs to be done in groups (task leader), groups seem to have similar structures (leader of the opposition), and people with different personalities want to behave in certain ways (social-emotional leader) while others play roles (like the joker or scapegoat) which enable them to present themselves as special or unique. There are a number of activities which groups deal with 'better' than individuals can. Some physical jobs require more than one person, to take an obvious example, and individuals can carry out specialist functions in taking on different aspects of a piece of work. In groups different people contribute different skills and knowledge so that groups can be 'better' at decision taking: members can criticise, stimulate and support one another in being committed to carrying out decisions. There are very different kinds of groups as we have seen, but they have common features:

1. the group norms
2. the roles that arise in a group
3. communications patterns within groups, and
4. the dynamics of group behaviour, the experience of the person in the group, and how this experience affects other members.

Groups have two aspects in that people join them primarily to carry out a task or pursue a leisure activity and because people want to interact with others, although the balance varies.

Parsons and Shils (1951) suggested that norms in any society or group must deal with four issues:

1. Are relations among members to be based on expression of the feelings they have about one another, or on the assumption that those feelings are to be suppressed?
2. Is involvement with one another to be total and unbounded (for example, as with parent and child), or is it to

be restricted and specific (as with doctor and patient)?
3. Is the significance of the other to be due to the unique relation one has with him (as brother or friend), or is it to be due to the fact that he represents a type or class of person (as a client or as an employer)?
4. Is the significance of the other to be due to his qualities (reliable, wise), or is it to be due to how he performs (as a teacher, surgeon)?

Some answers to these questions suggest that a contrast can be made between the traditional primary group, the family, where relations are based on expression of feelings, unique ties and high emotional involvement, and a professional or technical group like a surgical team, where relations are based on suppression of emotions, technical expertise and restricted involvement (Parsons and Shils, 1951). It is important to note that norms arise in a group without necessarily being articulated. Very few groups begin by stating their norms: often awareness of norms only occurs when they are breached. They seem to lie under the surface of social behaviour.

Norms may be classified as:

1. Those relating to the task; for example, the method, rate and standard of work in work teams. Deviation affects group goals and individual rewards.
2. Norms regulating interaction in the group which make the behaviour of others predictable, prevent conflicts, and ensure fair distribution of rewards.
3. Norms about attitudes and beliefs: the opinions of 'group experts' are accepted and beliefs are checked against those of the group rather than other people or experts outside the group who it may be made difficult to approach.
4. Norms about aspects of appearance, including clothes and hair, which project individual identity and may bring the group into disrepute.

It is possible for a minority of group members to change the norms. If one person in a group does not conform he or she can be dismissed as eccentric, but two or more people have to be taken more seriously if they express doubts. Change in groups will be dealt with shortly.

Certain sequences of interaction characteristically occur if group members do not conform. Members may deviate because they do not agree with, or approve of, a norm, or prefer a different way of doing things. Deviation is met with surprise and non-verbal and verbal signs of disapproval and, finally, rejection and exclusion from the group. Exceptions are made for people of high informal status in the group: they are given permission to deviate because of their contributions to the group. Their deviation is seen as an experimental course of action, but innovations are often made by defiant, uncompromising minorities rather than diplomatic, concilia-tory individuals. Norms help people to orientate themselves to each other by providing guidelines about how they should behave in relation to others.

Inter-group relations

We are uneasily aware of the tensions and conflicts between individuals, which have been studied by people like Bion. Inter-group relations is an area of group dynamics of special concern. Conflicts between groups may be due to economic, political, racial or religious differences, but knowing what underlies a problem does not necessarily lead to its ameliora-tion. Diagnoses and cures are not prerogatives of sociologists and social workers. We know that modifying group norms, values and behaviours is exceedingly difficult. However, the sociological study of groups can help us recognise that rivalries and hostilities between individuals (and also between groups) may be increased by some kinds of social organisation. Some groups are divided so as to utilise feelings of hostility and competitiveness on the rather crude assump-tion that competition between individuals or groups has the effect of 'improving' their performances or output. Workers or group members may experience conflicting feelings about this situation and, as a result, the competitive system may not work in the way intended. The people involved may then feel resentful, confused and insecure and become suspicious of the system as well as of each other.

To take one example, like many large institutions, a psychiatric hospital was re-organised into several small units which each had its own nurses, doctors and social workers. The way in which the hospital was re-organised aroused considerable anxiety among staff, who had had little preparation for the changes. Some of them resented the way they had been redeployed, but some people expressed a generalised feeling of grievance against 'them', or found particular people against whom to feel resentful. The social workers were able to express their feelings of frustration about poor co-ordination and communication to the principal social worker. They felt vulnerable since they sometimes perceived that responsibility was so diffuse that no one person or group was responsible for working for or with a particular patient. Perhaps as a result of their anxiety about what they perceived as a very fluid situation, they tended to adapt their work so as to fit in with the expectations of colleagues in their units. They changed their roles or added to them in order to conform to these expectations, but were seen as inconsistent or unreliable by some patients. One patient who had been in several of the units suggested that a case conference would help the staff 'to sort themselves out before trying to sort me out any more'. It proved to be a salutary experience for many members of staff when the principal social worker convinced them that the patient had a point, and the conference was convened.

The co-ordination of social work services in the hospital as a whole was the responsibility of the principal social worker, who was also attached to one of the units. He tried to encourage the social workers to have regular meetings, with the aim of reviewing work practices and of co-ordinating the use of resources and approaches to other organisations such as the Department of Health and Social Security and the Department of Employment. One long-serving social worker was able openly to express her misgivings about the way the hospital was run and the tensions in relationships among the social work staff. She decided not to attend the meetings, but was able to give the principal social worker support in other ways. The other social workers were not willing to do this, and used some meetings to discuss their feelings of resentment about other staff in the hospital and their attitudes to social work. The social workers experienced conflict around their attendance at the meetings and their loyalty to non-social work colleagues in their units. Other members of the hospital staff were curious about the meetings. Some felt threatened by them. One doctor asked the social worker on his unit not to discuss some aspects of their work, for example. However, the meetings did lead to some sharing of information and discussion of topics about which social workers felt concern, including issues about confidentiality and recording systems. Comparisons of work and work loads in different units provided a focus later, and members learned about differences in the kinds of referrals they received. There were fairly wide variations in the nature of referrals which appeared to reflect varying degrees of interest and understanding of social work among doctors and unit staff. The social workers said that they tended to look to the unit doctors for advice and direction about how to do their work, and it seemed that they felt threatened and insecure if the doctors were unable or unwilling to accept this role. For a time the meetings provided some mutual support, and the principal social worker was seen as a co-ordinator and facilitator. Feelings of competitiveness and distrust could be expressed in the group, and there were attempts to explore ways of co-operative working. However, the possibility of co-operative action was seen as directly at variance with the way in which staff perceived the unit system. The social workers began to absent themselves from meetings of the group or leave prematurely, and could not agree on ways to co-ordinate some aspects of their work. It thus appears that it was almost inevitable that they would be unable to form a group able to work together. An important factor in this seemed to be the conflict between the social workers' loyalties to their units and to the social work group.

This is one example of the way that a group is more likely to be successful if it is conducted in an organisation or institutional context in which other people, not directly involved with this group, nevertheless accept and support its aims and value its contribution to the goals of the institution or organisation (Whitaker, 1976). In thinking about starting a group, then, the social worker has to try to assess what the environment in which it will exist may be like. We have seen that a group which has an unhappy history or which has to contend with indifference or hostility within its own member-ship or from outside may be more difficult to maintain than a more internally cohesive group in a supportive environment. We may also use this illustration as an indication of some basic requirements of group work. For example, we need to remember that all members of one group are also likely to belong to others to which they may feel different degrees of loyalty. To support group work certain basic resources such as accommodation, equipment and finance, as well as staff, are needed. A period of negotiation may be needed to obtain these, and the example above shows that it may be a long time before a group can develop and work effectively.

Organisations as systems

The study of organisations is the study of particular groups: the essential problem of modern organisations is one of constructing groups to perform tasks effectively. Etzioni (1964) noted that organisations are characterised by division of labour and conscious planning, power relations and replaceable memberships. We have seen that the study of group dynamics and work groups should enable people to make constructive suggestions about effective organisation. They may be helped in this by assessing critically the assumptions on which welfare agencies are based and their taken-for-granted features. The ways in which sociologists look at organisations can be seen to correspond to the general theoretical positions in sociology outlines earlier. The approaches used in sociology, as we have seen, are not self-contained nor self-sufficient, and each theoretical position is only partial. It is inadvisable, then, to limit yourself to using one perspective rather than another. But social workers need to be aware of the theoretical and ideological origins of models of organisations.

To functionalists organisations, as social systems, are interpreted as being in a continuous process of adjusting to change in order to maintain their equilibrium. Their concern is with the ways the parts of system fit together, the functions the different parts perform for the whole, and with how the needs of systems are met. They are interested in how goals are defined and redefined, how the organisation adapts to change, and how group solidarity is preserved. Conflict theorists see conflict as central in groups and organisations. Functionalists acknowledge that strain is inevitably a feature of any social system. But for conflict theorists it is conflict and not the need for equilibrium which is the main source of change. They see power as the principal determinant of the forms taken by change. In any organisation, therefore, changes are to be analysed in terms of conflicting aims, interests and the distribution of power. Interactionists assume that organisations do not exist separately from definitions of them by their members and other people. They focus on the actions in a situation both as the constructions and as the interpreters of reality. An organisation is thus what its members make it or believe it to be. As we have noticed before, none of the approaches has completely solid empirical support, and they are each likely to have ideologically committed adherents.

Power and organisation structure

Social Services Departments are typically referred to as bureaucracies. This form of work group, as we have seen, is characterised among other things by a hierarchical authority structure based on official position rather than individualism. Sociological studies reveal a number of features commonly associated with the idea of professionalism. They are skill which is based on theoretical knowledge, a code of conduct, testing of the competence of members, the provision of training and education, and the rendering of an altruistic service. Sociologists have been concerned with the process by which an occupation becomes recognised as a profession. The sequence is that first a full-time occupation is created to provide a service and training is established. Next, a professional association is formed and the formal code of ethics is evolved. In his study of social work organisations, Smith

(1970) examined the way in which professional persons who work within bureaucratic organisations are subject to socially-structured tensions which are particularly acute. He suggested that some features of the social work profession, including their low professional status and their resultant impaired ability to claim professional autonomy, highlight the tension between organisational bureaucratisation and the professionalisation of social work. A systematic division of labour, rights and power is thought to be essential for rational organisation. Each staff member needs to know his work and have the resources to carry it out. He or she must also know the limitations of their work so as not to overstep their boundaries and thus undermine the system. Each of the hierarchy is supervised by a higher member so that no position is left uncontrolled. Rules are seen to be important in supposedly aiding rational and consistent treatment. They economise effort, since new solutions do not have to be found for each new problem or case. They are supposed to facilitate standard practice and equality in the treatment of many cases.

Studies of bureaucracies have often focused on the nature of the rules in organisations. The bureaucrat has been seen as conforming to formal rules or else as acting in terms of a system of rules that members use to describe and account for their activity (rather than seeing behaviour as governing by rules). Paradoxically, a rule may be violated, but this activity is still justified with reference to the rule. Zimmerman (1971) studied behaviour in a US Bureau of Public Assistance. Clients applying for help were assigned to caseworkers by receptionists. Officially, the procedure was governed by the simple rule that the first four clients who arrived were assigned one to each caseworker. The next four clients were assigned in a similar manner, but from time to time the rule was broken. A caseworker may have had a difficult case and the interview may have lasted much longer than the average. In this situation a receptionist might reorganise the assignment list and switch the next client to another caseworker. Such rule violations were explained by receptionists in terms of the rule. In their eyes, by breaking the rule they were conforming to the rule. From their point of view the rule was intended to keep clients moving with a minimum of delay so that they had all been attended to by the end of the day. Violating the rule to ensure this result could be explained as following the rule, and the receptionists could explain the paradox and justify their actions to themselves and to others. By seeing their actions as conforming to a rule they created an appearance of order. Rather than being simply directed by rules, Zimmerman argues that the receptionists were constantly monitoring and assessing the situation and adapting their behaviour to what they saw as the requirements of the situation. The use of rules by members to describe and account for their actions makes social situations seem orderly for the participants. It is this sense and appearance of order that rules in use, in fact, provide. This study illustrates the reflexive nature of the procedures used by members to construct an appearance of order. Receptionists interpret their activity as evidence of an underlying pattern – the intent of the rule, and see particular actions, even when they break the rules, as evidence of the underlying pattern.

From an interactionist point of view, action is not necessarily determined in a simple way by external forces, but rather is directed instead by the meanings which actors give to events and to the activities of themselves and others. Action arises out of meanings which define social reality. For example, a number of meanings may be given to an instruction or order issued by a manager. A worker may see it as reasonable, may regard obedience as demeaning, or involving no loss of self-respect. As a result of the meaning attributed to it, it may be obeyed willingly or reluctantly, it may be ignored or refused. To understand the worker's response it is necessary to discover the meanings which influence it. It may be seen by a subordinate, or by field or residential workers as reasonable or unreasonable. Complying with the instruction could be regarded as demeaning, in which case you have to weigh the possible consequences of not carrying it out with how strongly you react to it personally and professionally. Discussion with other social workers in a team is often advisable if it is not unavoidable in these circumstances. It is advisable because even if others have not received similar instructions their views may help you to consider other perspectives or strategies. It is also advisable because of the value of group support. An individual may be more easily dealt with by supervisors, and it can be arduous and unproductive as well as self-destructive to 'go it alone' unless there really are no alternatives or possibilities of compromise. A united group of workers or a cohesive area team is a very different proposition for management to deal with. Payne (1982) has pointed out that teamwork is like any other form of organisation in being an instrument for carrying out policy; that is, as a way of getting workers to do what the management of an organisation wants. Many social workers nevertheless see teamwork as a form of mutual support, and as a way of influencing managers to do what they want.

Some characteristics of bureaucracy have been seen as particularly related to social work organisations. A particular feature is the hierarchical authority structure based on official positions. The rights and duties of occupants of these positions are set down in codes of rules and regulations. In bureacracies labour is highly specialised and clearly divided between tasks. Relationships between staff are impersonal in nature, and management is based on written documents. Some aspects of bureaucratic procedurte may be dysfunctional to an organisation. In particular, they may encourage behaviour which inhibits the attainment of the organisation's goals. The bureaucrat is trained to comply strictly with the rules, but when situations arise that are not covered by the rules this training may lead to inflexibility and failure to use initiative, as the bureaucrat is not taught to improvise and innovate. It may not be in his interest to bend the rules, even when this may further the realisation of organisational goals. There is a tendency for conformity to official regulations to become an end in itself rather than a means to an end. The bureaucrat may lose sight of the goals of the organisation, and 'red tape' may stand in the way of providing an efficient service for the organisation's clients.

Bureaucratic procedures emphasise impersonality, and this may lead to friction between the staff of the organisation and the public. Whereas clients may expect concern and sympathy, the impartial and 'business-like' treatment they receive leads to bureaucrats being seen as cold, abrupt anu unsympathetic. As a result, clients sometimes feel that thcy have been badly served by bureacracies, a finding confirmed by some consumer studies of social services. There are social class variations in the ways people perceive social services and how easily they make use of them. The majority of the most persistent social problems dealt with by welfare services are found in families where the bread-winner is unemployed or in unskilled manual work. Most of those who might be expected to use the services of social agencies come from working-class cultural backgrounds. But most social service organisations operate in ways which are rooted in middle-class values and ways of doing things. Thus it has been argued that welfare bureaucracies encounter difficulties in coping with lower-class groups, and their policies may actually reinforce the clients' culture of deprivation. It has been observed that lower-class clients lack the skills needed in coping with complex organisations. They have difficulties in dealing with the technicalities of rights, procedures and impersonal routines and in relating to officials. Clients do not always present their problems in ways which fit in with established categories for which there are clear action guidelines.

This reference to clients' views on the service they receive underlines the importance of the ways social services organisations deal with people who approach them for help. This has been recognised in discussion of intake interviews. I would now like to give attention to other aspects of the process of becoming a client. Social work agencies tend to divide the way new clients are dealt with into: (a) reception, which is an intitial screening usually by clerical or secretarial staff; (b) intake, an intitial interview with a social worker, some aspects of which will be discussed later; and (c) allocation, when a 'case' is taken on for work by the agency's staff. It is usually recognised that a number of jobs such as clerk, typist and receptionist are extremely important in bureaucratic organisations. It has, however, been assumed that their functions are passive, and so their influence on the agency and its clients is not much examined. Assumptions like these are questioned in a study of reception processes reported by Hall (1974). He found that untrained receptionists, often without privacy for interviews, requested information about personal problems, and decided whether a client could be seen, when and by whom. Reception staff are responsible, in effect, for the regulation of 'bombardment' of social work staff. How they do this varies according to the receptionist involved and the attitude of the client. Most commonly they explain to the client that the social worker they wish to see is not available until a particular time, and suggest that the client should wait or call back later.

From the clients' point of view, perhaps the most important consideration is the ability and willingness of reception staff to act as advocates on their behalf in contracts with social work staff. When clients are not seen promptly by social workers, receptionists frequently telephone them again (often stressing urgency) to ensure that clients are seen as quickly as possible. To a large extent the receptionists' willingness to act as advocates for the clients in this way is related to their own assessment of the needs of the clients or on whether they personally like or dislike certain individuals. After the receptionist has conducted the initial interview to establish the reason for the client's visit, the telephone call to the social worker may stress the urgency of the problem in an attempt to ensure that the client is seen. On the other hand, clients can be suppressed in various ways. The conversation between the receptionist and the social worker may under-state the problem and result in delay before the client is seen.

Reception staff are constantly faced with the problem of dealing with clients when a social worker is not available to see them. They may try to provide a service themselves, or attempt to ensure that the social worker sees the client as soon as possible. The receptionist may advise a client to go to another agency or provide advice and assistance on the problem facing the client. When a client has explained the problems to the receptionist and a social worker is not available, the advisory role would seem to be a logical or natural reaction on the part of the receptionist. This informal extension of their discretionary powers may serve to increase job satisfaction, although it may give rise to further problems for the social worker and the agency. For some workers the existence of receptionists allows them to delegate certain responsibilities which, for various reasons, they feel unable to meet. Social workers may tend to place a considerable amount of the responsibility for clients visiting the agency on the receptionists. This often gives rise to considerable problems in relationships between social workers and reception staff. In the opinion of the receptionist the client may be being treated unfairly by the social worker. The extent to which receptionists can influence social workers is limited in a relationship in which they are subordinate. This may lead to the receptionists trying to provide a service which they may think is really the social worker's job.

The work of a federal law enforcement agency in the USA was studied by Blau (1963). Agents were employed to inspect businesses to determine whether laws dealing with standards of employment were being observed. The laws involved were very detailed, and it was often difficult for the agents to decide how they applied to particular cases. Officially such difficulties should be discussed with the supervisor, but agents were often reluctant to do this because their promotion prospects depended largely on his evaluation of their work and frequent consultation might indicate incompetence. So, in direct violation of the official rules, they sought advice and guidance from each other. Blau claimed that this unofficial consultation helped increase the agents' efficiency. They shared information and experience, and this facilitated problem solving. Their anxiety about making decisions, for example about whether or not to prosecute a company, was reduced because they knew they could rely on their colleagues' advice. Blau concluded that, paradoxically, unofficial practices explicitly prohibited by official regulations could sometimes further the achievement of organisational objectives. He argued that no system of official rules and supervision could anticipate all the problems which may arise in an organisation. Efficiency can be maximised by the development of informal work norms by groups of workers, and such norms influence the efficiency of the organisation.

Conclusion

Groups are important topics in sociology because they are the units through which social life is organised. There are many kinds of groups, and they have different structures which affect the behaviour of members. Primary groups are usually small, and members are in face-to-face communication with one another. They are the groups in which people seek to have their basic physical and psychological needs met. As social organisations families are obvious examples of primary groups, and they too vary widely. The study of different kinds of family units in different societies has been a popular area of work for sociologists and anthropologists for many years. In all societies some kind of family exists, but in different societies and at different times a very wide range of behaviour, structure and attitudes is found. Child rearing, for example, is in some cases shared between mothers and fathers, in other cases it is a wider communal responsibility, and in yet others it is seen to be the responsibility of mothers. We noted that the groups to which people belong in everyday life are important sources of self-esteem as well as imposing pressure on individuals. Systems theories provide a way of thinking about the structure of groups and about relationships between group members, and we have noted that the concept of role is important to systems theorists. It is used in describing the ways people adapt to being group members and how they relate to one another. Conflict of various kinds is an important aspect of group dynamics, and there are complex relationships between group norms, change in groups and among their members. Psycho-analytic thinking has contributed to understanding group dynamics and the intense feelings that energise them, and the tensions found in relations between groups. We noted that secondary groups are more impersonal and generally larger than primary groups, and that the essential problem of modern organisations is goal attainment rather than meeting members' needs. Formal organisations or bureaucracies are large groups which have explicit goals and procedures and an emphasis on the jobs people do rather than particular individuals. This is the form of organisation usually associated with social services, and sociological studies have focused on tensions between professional discretion, administrative requirements and power in organisations and critical assessment of assumptions on which welfare agencies are based.

4

Social Work Practice: Individuals and Families

Cultural influences and family interaction

The need for social workers to have some understanding of cultural influences on behaviour and on the interaction between family members rather than focusing exclusively on one individual is seen in work with members of ethnic minorities. In making assessments social workers need to bear in mind the cultural dimension found throughout social work. Cultural differences between clients and social workers are important if they are of the same nationality. They require careful consideration too if they are of different nationality or ethnic origin. Social workers need to look at their moral and intellectual adequacy with minority groups. Social workers need to have some understanding of clients' family and social networks, and their values and past and present experiences. For example, one needs to discover if the client is part of a family, what the pattern of obligations and responsibilities is, and the roles of the head and other members. To whom would the client be expected to defer? Who would be expected to defer to the client? How are children cared for? What personality characteristics are highly valued? The social worker needs to gain insights into how people see the reasons for their problems and explain them to themselves. The need to understand clients' networks and relationships can be illustrated by referring to work with West Indian people. Quite often it is unnecessary to admit children to care if the social worker takes account of the family and neighbourhood. Quite often there are relatives and friends who will care for children. Caution is therefore necessary in making assumptions about immigrants' ways of life, and in too readily assuming that they lack social support. Emigration from their home affects relationships between West Indian men and women in that the demands made on them in Britain can provoke the expression of their mutual ambivalence. Husbands and wives have to rely more on each other for material support, but if they have grown up in matriarchal families they may feel uncertain about male and female roles when they enter a society where these roles are changing. Some West Indian women may be ambivalent about men's ability to support them and may thus contribute to their husband's dependence on them. Awareness of the more equal relationship between wives and husbands in Britain may lead West Indian wives to resent their husbands' attempts to dominate their families and to criticise them for not taking greater responsibility for the upbringing and care of their children. Even in some families where the father's patriarchal role seems well established and is unchallenged by the mother, it usually does not survive the questioning and revolt of the children. In bringing up their children West Indian parents will draw on their own experience and will tend to enforce discipline by external sanctions and threats, which may appear harsh to British eyes. This may reflect the West Indians' anxiety for their children to be seen as respectable. The British may not understand this, nor that the pattern of life of many West Indian families is a complex mixture of working-class and middle-class customs and attitudes. They may see a West Indian family as working class whereas the family may see themselves as middle class.

Social workers should therefore carefully seek advice from members of the clients' culture for information about clients' problems and responses to them, and for ideas about possible help. The social worker in any given case should try to find out what effect his or her age, sex, class and other characteristics may have on the client. The usefulness of casework help to ethnic minority people with personal and relationship problems cannot be taken for granted. When it is undertaken, social workers need insight into their own cultural identity, the clients and their cultural identity, and how these will influence the casework relationship. The cultural dimension is present whether the social worker is arranging day care, trying to improve housing conditions or looking for foster parents. Above all, stereotyped judgements about the psycho-social functioning of ethnic minority clients have to be avoided. These examples of areas for enquiry are discussed quite fully elsewhere (see Saifullah Khan, 1979; Cheetham, 1982). In working with people who are immigrants and refugees it is advisable to bear in mind that their experience of officials has probably been distressing. It may be hard to develop a relationship of trust, and refugees may be uneasy about giving information about themselves. They may have learned to tell their stories in a superficial way to such people as immigration officials, teachers and doctors. In addition to knowledge about culture, social workers will see knowledge about separation and loss as a key in this work. I think there is widespread concern, not only among social workers but certainly including them, that professional services for the members of minority groups are inadequate. Cheetham (1982), whose book on the subject is a useful source for social workers, says that there is a need for us to become yet more aware of racist attitudes and the racist structures within which we operate.

Family disorganisation and violence

Sociology also contributes to an understanding of the processes underlying family problems and the identification of areas of family life that give rise to disorganisation and crisis. It is thus of help to social workers in assessing family problems and suggesting methods of intervention. As far as class differences in violent behaviour are concerned, it has been argued that its incidence among husbands in professional and managerial strata is markedly below that of other occupational levels. The available evidence, it was said, suggests that although frustration and stress occur in any social class, people with low incomes and poor education have fewer resources to cope with stress when it rises than those who are thought to be more privileged. McKinley (1964) did not find it surprising that the perceived incidence of violence is greatest among the most socially disadvantaged. Insofar as violent behaviour is learned, it seemed that couples where both partners have grown up in middle-class homes are less likely to have witnessed physical violence between their parents than is the case in marriages where one or both partners are of working-class origin. These generalisations need to be treated with caution. It also needs to be remembered that psychological abuse which has long term and serious ill effects may occur in families. Thus more research is needed on middle-class families where this may occur, as well as working-class families. I shall later refer also to the ways in which problems are socially defined and the issues which this raises. It used to be assumed that violence in families could be 'explained' by reference to 'personality disorder' or individual pathology. Sociological studies have suggested that these are partial 'explanations' which apply only to some cases. Not all of the husbands and fathers who are violent are mentally ill, and there is evidence to show that some violent behaviour is learned. Couples who have seen their parents behave violently are more likely to be violent, or expect to be violent, in their own marriages, than couples who have had non-violent parental models. Children of violent parents learn that violence is a 'normal' response to stress. Violence is thought to be a result of socialisation in violent homes. It has been suggested that men who are relatively disadvantaged and whose ambitions are unfulfilled are more prone to violence. Feeling failures as breadwinners, these husbands may assert themselves in violent ways to compensate for lack of money and respect. Anxiety about their status as heads of families also arises when wives bring most resources to marriages because they are better educated and have higher status jobs, and this may lead husbands to try to assert their authority through violence.

A variety of factors are put forward as causes of marital violence but authorities vary in what they emphasise. As we have seen, some stress individual characteristics of the personalities and the importance of alcohol. Some seek to bridge social structural and pathological factors. They suggest that men resort to violence when they feel they lack the personal resources to meet cultural expectations of superior patriarchal status (Good, 1971; Dobash and Dobash, 1980). These explanations, however, do not say precisely how cultural and sociological factors interact with individual behaviour, and this difficulty may lead practitioners to favour individual rather than cultural explanations. Explanations based on individual personality are easier to grasp, though they may not be more accurate. Doctors, health visitors and social workers believe that explanations are necessary in order to diagnose problems and decide on treatment. They believe that they should obtain evidence, define marital violence as an abnormal problem, explain it as a reaction to stress, as due to personality problems, drink or drugs, and then decide what kind of help offers the best chance of cure or prevention in the light of available skills, knowledge and agency function. But you can argue that it is wrong to assume that practitioners stand apart from the patients' situation, and that it is more realistic to see the practitioner as part of the situation being diagnosed. A client's social circumstances may be altered by the fact that the practitioner is defining, attaching meaning to, and explaining them. The kind of service that clients approach may well influence the way they present their problems, and practitioners probably 'invent' explanations in order to convince themselves that marital violence is abnormal when in fact it might not be (Borkowski, Murch and Walker, 1983). The evidence available about family violence does not permit firm conclusions to be drawn. But it is known that violence to children occurs in situations of stress, frustration, social isolation, disadvantage and person- ality problems: one or more of these may be evident, but it is not known which variables are crucial in leading to child abuse. In the NSPCC study (Baher, 1974), most abused children were unwanted at the time of birth, and children most at risk were the results of unwanted pregnancies when mothers had been refused abortions, and they were often unresponsive to their babies from birth. When normal bonding between mothers and children does not occur, for whatever the reason, it is less likely that the mothers will be able to tolerate the tedium of child care, and they will make unrealistic demands on immature children. Once poor parent-child relationships are established and have led to violence, it is likely to be a cumulative process and relationships become steadily worse.

Ways of helping abusing parents are varied. One aim is to try to reinforce parents' positive reactions to their children. They are encouraged to improve communication between themselves and their children, giving children positive attention and having expectations and making demands appropriate to their ages. Parents are encouraged to learn new ways of handling children, for example by distracting them, calming arguments by refusing to raise their voices, and by considering the appropriateness of behaviour (for example, in relation to children's ages) before punishing. Another method is enlisting the help of other people in improving children's behaviour. This may help parents to see that children's behaviour can improve, at the same time relieving them of the burden of producing change and having complete responsibility for trying to do this (Jeffrey, 1976). Group methods may be helpful to violent parents either in themselves or in conjunction with individual counselling. Groups organised by parents themselves such as Parents Anonymous can provide reassurance to people who mistrust help from official agencies. It has been found that members feel less inhibited in discussing and coming to terms with their feelings about their children and their experiences. They are often able to confront each other and to share ideas about possible solutions to family problems. These kinds of mutual help groups may have the services of social workers who may support new members who are more emotionally disturbed than others recognise, and may also follow up anyone who seems particularly distressed by a discussion. Other groups may be led by professionals who might help members to discuss early difficulties they find in relating positively to others about whom they have conflicting feelings (Kempe and Kempe, 1978).

Minority groups and personal change

In working with ethnic and perhaps other minority groups, social workers are aware that they may be regarded suspiciously as potential sources of discrimination. These suspicions may decrease as relationships develop but may never completely disappear. They may not be expressed openly although people may show signs of thinking that they are given inferior service. If they avoid discussing this, social workers and their clients may be left feeling resentful and uncomfortable. Discussion in itself does not necessarily lead to the disappearance of painful feelings, but if they are not recognised there is a greater chance of their remaining an obstacle. Usually the more effective approach to dealing with prejudice is indirect and involves focusing on and taking seriously factors thought to contribute to the insecurity of groups or individuals. Sometimes it is possible to reduce tensions only by dealing with these factors and by gaining the confidence of leaders who may still be insecure. They are more likely to identify the problems they have in common with those towards whom they feel antagonistic, and also to act in ways which will protect their own interests without undermining those of other people. Life planning and personal re-evaluation workshops have been used to help individuals to manage personal change. An assumption underlying this approach is that the individual's concept of self organises the way self is seen in relation to the world, and that it also spurs the individual to action. Throughout their lives individuals will search for ways to play the kind of roles which are in harmony both with the way in which they see themselves, and the way they would like to be seen. When deprived of work, the individual's concept of self is sabotaged and he or she is in danger of losing his or her sense of purpose. Life planning and personal re-evaluation help people to re-examine themselves and use the resulting revised concepts of self to develop new goals. Workshops provide a framework for people, alone and in groups, to answer such questions as:

Who am I and where am I now?
How did I get here?
How satisfied am I with who I am and where I am?
How would I like to change my life and myself?
How rational are these wishes?
How do I achieve these aims?

Life planning and personal re-evaluation aims to: (i) further understanding of one's behaviour and possible reasons for it; (ii) help in coping with negative feelings more effectively through feeling more positive about oneself; and (iii) achieve changes in observable behaviour, for example, creating or taking opportunities (Hopson, 1976). It may not always be desirable or possible to help people develop new or more appropriate self concepts, but methods of this kind may be used in relation to various situations, retirement being one example. It offers a way to encourage people to think positively and to plan for retirement.

Interactionist approaches

Interactionist approaches differ from functionalist and systems theories and emphasise individuals' views and interpretations of social reality. Crucial to these perspectives in sociology are the 'meanings' that people give to situations and the ways they interpret actions. Basically, they are grounded on the assumption that there is no such thing as a single social reality. There are many different constructions which depend on the identities of the different people involved and on the context in which they occur. The following discussion is based on tape-recorded excerpts from an interview between a client, Mrs Smith, and a social worker, from a discussion about some aspects of that interview between the social worker and myself. This material suggests different interpretations of the situation, information gained in the discussion with the social worker providing new ideas about the original interview. The views of the different people involved indicate that it is helpful to take into account the organisational context of the interviews. The social workers and I listened to the tape recordings of their interviews with clients and then discussed what happened and their views on what clients said. These discussions were also recorded on tape. I am thus concerned with some difficult fundamental questions about interviewing methods and styles and the ways in which conceptual frameworks and organisational contexts influence the thinking of social workers. The first excerpt is from an

interview with Mrs Smith after she had written to the Social
Services Department asking to be registered as a physically
handicapped person. The people involved consented to the
recordings being made, of course, and they have been edited
to the extent necessary to protect their privacy.

*Excerpt from an interview between Mrs Smith and Social
Worker*

Social Worker	You contacted the department because you'd like to be registered physically handicapped.
Mrs Smith	Mmmm.
Social Worker	Can you tell me a little more about your condition?
Mrs Smith	Arthritis in both knees.
Social Worker	Yes.
Mrs Smith	And I'm on tablets, four of one sort and six of another, every day.
Social Worker	For your arthritis?
Mrs Smith	Yes. But I had an infection on my feet and its only since the end of October that I've been able to walk about.
Social Worker	Yes.
Mrs Smith	But that, they reckon, was due to the shock of losing my husband you see in March.
Social Worker	In March last year?
Mrs Smith	Yes. But I can't get out. Some days I haven't been able to walk (mumble). The doctor says there's too much weight and wear and tear on my knees – get your weight down.
Social Worker	Yes. What about things like housework and getting about now?
Mrs Smith	I have some help.
Social Worker	Yes.
Mrs Smith	And a bath nurse.
Social Worker	And how often do they come?
Mrs Smith	The home help comes three mornings a week and the nurse comes every Monday.
Social Worker	Yes. . . . So it's walking that is your. . . .

Mrs Smith	It's walking, getting about you see.
Social Worker	What about shopping?
Mrs Smith	Well, on a Thursday as a rule, a friend across the road – providing he's all right for driving, 'cos he's not A1 in health.
Social Worker	Yes.
Mrs Smith	He takes me there and takes me home. If I try to walk about too much I've had it.
Social Worker	Have you lived here long?
Mrs Smith	Since 'seventy-four.
Social Worker	I think you're from the South?
Mrs Smith	Yes, from London.
Social Worker	Yes. And how long were you and your husband married?
Mrs Smith	Seven years.
Social Worker	And did he die very suddenly?
Mrs Smith	Well, he'd been ill for a long while, going downhill, put it that way, for a long while. And then he was bad in the January. We took him to my daughter but he took worse there. We brought him back and got him into hospital. Then he died in March.
Social Worker	So it was quite a shock for you?
Mrs Smith	Well it was because you see we've never been apart.
Social Worker	You were a very close couple. . . .
Mrs Smith	Oh we were very, very close. Those few years were the happiest in my life.
Social Worker	Have you any family Mrs Smith?
Mrs Smith	Yes, I've got eight.
Social Worker	Eight children. Are any of them near at hand?
Mrs Smith	There's one in (mumble) but she does not know she's got a mother.
Social Worker	You mean there's no contact between you? That's very sad. Is there any reason for that?
Mrs Smith	I don't know. Not on my part there's not. But she is that way. She is temperamental that way. If she runs into trouble she'll know where I am.

Social Worker	So how long is it since you've seen her?
Mrs Smith	Eh. Must have been August time.
Social Worker	That's very sad isn't it?
Mrs Smith	There's another one.
Social Worker	And do you have any contact with her?
Mrs Smith	Oh she's more of a daughter. Oh yes, I've only got to pick up the 'phone and say I'm fed up, I'm feeling down, can I come through. What train are you coming on mum? Just give me time to get to the station. Yes, I can be through there as long as I like.
Social Worker	That's nice.
Mrs Smith	My daughter was here at the weekend and she said 'Can you do me a favour?' I said 'Well if I can, you know I will. 'Well', she says, 'can you wash John's coat?' He's only five, bless him, and she's only got the one coat for him for school, so I said 'Course I can girl. I says 'You know that'.
Social Worker	I see. You see quite a lot of them.
Mrs Smith	Oh yes, they get through here or I get through there.
Social Worker	Do you find that your arthritis causes you any problems going up the stairs?
Mrs Smith	Well it does, but I just take me time. Go up one step at a time. Or if it's too bad then I'll sit down and work meself up that way. . . .
Social Worker	The doctor suggested that you might try to lose a little weight. Have you tried that?
Mrs Smith	I've already lost a lot.
Social Worker	You have – and what have you been doing to lose that then?
Mrs Smith	Starving myself. . . .
Social Worker	What sort of things have you cut down on?
Mrs Smith	Sugar and sweets. I've cut down on potatoes.
Social Worker	Do you cook for yourself?
Mrs Smith	Sometimes. Not every day.
Social Worker	Why?
Mrs Smith	Can't be bothered.
Social Worker	And what do you do in your spare time? Do

you knit or sew?

Mrs Smith   I make all sorts of things. I'll show you a suitcase. I've got a suitcase out there with it in.

Comment

There are various ways in which the information given in this excerpt might be interpreted. Additional evidence, about non-verbal behaviour or facial expression, for example, could lead to different interpretations than those based on the tape recording alone. An interpretation based on the excerpt above might be as follows. The arthritis does involve problems for Mrs Smith but she seems to be able to cope with them. For example, she finds ways of negotiating stairs, and she appears to have sufficient help at home from the home help and the nurse. She sees quite a lot of them. In addition, she has the help of the neighbour with her shopping. The doctor has advised her about the need to lose weight and if she does this her mobility may improve. Mrs Smith has a number of relatives and although it seems that she is not on good terms with one daughter and has little contact with her, there is another who is described as 'more of a daughter'. Mrs Smith is able to telephone her and can visit her. This daughter visited Mrs Smith recently and it seems that Mrs Smith was pleased to be asked to wash her grandson's coat. She also derives satisfaction from sewing and knitting and took pride in showing the social worker the things she had made. At the moment, then, there are no clearly defined needs for practical or material help, and there does not seem to be justification for further contact on the part of the social worker, who can now complete the application for registration.

One outcome of such an interpretation could be to recommend no further action and to close the file. But there could be other ways of looking at the situation. Other information, for example, could lead to different assessments of Mrs Smith's situation. Also, other social workers with different ideas about initial interviews and with different perspectives on social work intervention might react differently. Thirdly, staff in other positions in the department were found to have different views about the social worker's actions. The first of these points is illustrated vividly by the discussion between the social worker and myself. This shows how additional information may make it possible to arrive at a different interpretation or develop different ideas. It indicated that in addition to the presenting problem or task, the social worker construed other dimensions in Mrs Smith's experience and possible 'needs' for continuing social work intervention.

Excerpt from the discussion of the interview with the Social Worker

Peter R. Day   How did the interview begin?

Social Worker   We talked about the arthritis and came to the conclusion that the main problem was walking and getting about.

Peter R. Day   Then there was a change of subject. What was in your mind?

Social Worker   In my mind then was trying to establish what sort of contacts this lady had made in the area, because that often gives you a clue as to how they relate socially, and in her case it seemed to me that she had made one or two nearby contacts but in fact that she's a relative stranger in her area, the fact that her relatives are scattered about and therefore the loneliness is more acute. She is still really grieving for her husband and clearly they were very close. She's really now beginning to feel the full effects of being alone. Because of the ice and snow she could not get to her daughter, and apart from an outing for lunch she said this would have been the very first Christmas she had ever spent alone. And she clearly felt that quite acutely.

Peter R. Day   You also asked her about how long she'd been married and about whether her husband died suddenly.

Social Worker   Yes, because I noticed a picture on the wall with her husband's name on, that she had painted herself. She had not told me in her letter that her husband was in fact her third husband and that he'd died last March. That brought it home to me that she's still really within the grieving process because she spoke very fondly of him and clearly he was very close to her. And she's really now beginning to feel the full effects of being alone. She talked about this even after the recording, that because of the snowy weather she couldn't get to her daughters.

Peter R. Day   Earlier on she described the marriage as the happiest years of her life. Were there other clues about her feeling lonely?

Social Worker   Yes. . . . she used the what I call the 'don't go yet' or delaying tactic. She brought out the things she had made. . . . insisted on going through the whole suitcase and I admired them – they were, you know, super things: she knits quite fiddly patterns and she sews a lot. If I've got any spare wool I said I'd give it to her.

Peter R. Day   What does the grieving process mean to you?

Social Worker   It means to me a situation in which my experience has taught me that what tends to happen is that at the very beginning when death is experienced they're looked after very well by the relatives and there is the funeral and they're looked after very well, get lots of visits from people, friendly neighbours, family, etcetera, and they appear then to have come to terms with the loss, but I believe it takes obviously considerably longer than that. She told me it was a very close and loving relationship with her husband. Reaching the time of their lives when they could enjoy each other's company without the children. To someone like her that

process is still going on because I think from the way she talked she was looking forward to their retirement years together and all the things they would be able to do together.

Peter R. Day   After you asked about contact with relatives and Mrs Smith replied, you said that's very sad. What was your reason for saying that?

Social Worker   That estate on which she lives is fairly isolated from the main town. I immediately thought well if she's got a daughter who lives that close to her she would be the one that would be supporting her mother, but it then transpired that there had been some rift between them.

Peter R. Day   Yes. Why did you say it was very sad?

Social Worker   Well, I think because her facial expression and gestures at the time I found very significant, in as much that I felt although I didn't explore that particular avenue, that the sort of rejection or cut-off by this particular daughter was of some considerable significance and that she felt it very, very keenly indeed. She looked very despondent and quite a bitter look came over her face, as though she felt that here was a time of need when she could perhaps have relied on her daughter for support.

Peter R. Day   You then changed the subject, asking about managing the stairs.

Social Worker   Yes.

Peter R. Day   That was a deliberate change of subject was it?

Social Worker   Yes, it was a deliberate change of subject because I just felt, again by her facial expressions and gestures, that the subject of her family and the possible lack of contact was quite a painful subject to her and that perhaps in subsequent interviews with her this is something that I could explore, but I feel that when you are making a new relationship with somebody it is all right to touch on the very difficult areas but it isn't always a wise thing to keep homing in on that same topic. I then try and allow the client to return to it if they feel they want to, but in her case I think too in an initial interview like that where they feel that you have got something they might want, such as entry into a different social (mumble) increasing her mobility, they occasionally feel that little bit embarrassed that they have let slip or let you see a part of their lives which they are not particularly proud of. And I feel that there must be an awful lot in the relationships which she has with her family which she isn't too happy about. And she feels isolated on the estate. So she seemed grateful when I returned to the somewhat safer ground of her disability.

Peter R. Day   After that there was another change of subject.

Social Worker   What I was really trying to find out is, you know, here we have a woman who has lost her husband fairly recently. It appears that there is only one family member of any significance that offers her any support. I just found myself wondering here's a woman with an awful lot of time on her hands to brood and get depressed about her situation. So I wanted to try and find out what she did with the time.

Peter R. Day   What kind of picture were you getting?

Social Worker   I was concerned that what I was getting was a very negative, depressed picture, the difficulty with the relatives, the social isolation, the fact that she can't get about very much, the fact that she doesn't have a lot of contact with people. I think too that she was feeling that perhaps she was presenting a depressed, negative picture. Then we went on to talk

	about a social club or a craft club of some kind.
Peter R. Day	Did you feel that she made you feel depressed?
Social Worker	Did she make me feel depressed? No. . . . no, I think the only depressing note I found was that, er, if she had not contacted us by letter er, it could have then gone on to, I think, the sort of depression where she would need to go to the doctor. It all made me wonder that obviously there's more to it than just the medical problem with which she first presented.
Peter R. Day	Arthritis, making her feel frustrated.
Social Worker	That's so, but in fact with Mrs Smith it is the isolation of her situation, the lack of contact with other people. She is obviously feeling that isolation keenly on this new estate.
Peter R. Day	Did you feel the same kind of way in some sense in picking up these cues from her?
Social Worker	No. I think what I did feel is that there must be many more people in a similar situation on that particular estate who haven't been able to communicate this sense of loneliness.

Comment

The information which the social worker gives during this discussion serves to amplify the picture of Mrs Smith and her situation. It indicates that the social worker's evidence leads her to interpret the situation in a way which is different from the comment above. Mrs Smith does not state explicitly that she feels lonely in her interview with the social worker. But in discussing the interview there is an early reference by the social worker to the loneliness being acute: Mrs Smith is said to be really 'beginning to feel the full effects of being alone'. The discussion of the interview indicates that the social worker began to explore the extent of Mrs Smith's social contacts. The social worker seems to have formed the impression that Mrs Smith might have been rather isolated socially and she questioned how Mrs Smith felt about this. It seemed from the client's facial expression and gestures that this question of lack of social contact could have been painful or difficult. For this reason the social worker deliberately guided the conversation away from this subject but noted that this could be explored in later interviews. There is thus a tacit assumption that this will not be a single interview.

The social worker sees the arthritis as leading to problems of mobility for the client, and refers to Mrs Smith's feelings about not being able to get to her daughter in snowy weather. The social worker is uncertain whether her daughter visits her very much and she seems to have the impression that it is Mrs Smith who has to initiate contact by telephoning her daughter. Perhaps if she is physically capable Mrs Smith is able to visit her daughter. But it is open to question how the client feels about herself if she has to initiate contact each time and take the role of visitor. It seems clear from the discussion that the social worker perceives a need for more information about her client's possible social isolation, and recognises that some of the evidence is ambiguous, and susceptible to different interpretations. For example, when Mrs Smith showed the social worker the things she had made this could indicate satisfaction with personal achievement and thus a positive indication of self-esteem. Or, as the social worker said, it could indicate more negative feelings of depression and the associated poor self-esteem. The discussion with the social worker provides several pieces of information which give clues to whether Mrs Smith is lonely, to her relationships with other people and how she feels about herself. The social worker comments that Mrs Smith is a relative stranger in the area and that she has not finished grieving for her husband. She bases this partly on the way Mrs Smith talked about her husband and said that clearly he was very close to her. She notes that she did not explore very far Mrs Smith's feelings of being rejected by her daughter: 'she felt it very keenly indeed.' The social worker comments on there being only one member of her family who gives Mrs Smith any kind of support, in the fact that she is not very mobile and does not have very much contact with people, and that the estate is fairly isolated from the main town.

In seeking to understand Mrs Smith's situation and her attitudes to it the social worker seems to have found it helpful to distinguish social isolation, which may be assessed in terms of the network of people with whom the client had contact, and loneliness, Mrs Smith's subjective experience. It seems very important to recognise that loneliness is a self-perceived problem. It involves awareness of lack of warmth and human contact often accompanied by feelings of low self-esteem. Many people have this experience but people who are elderly, disabled and widowed can be particularly vulnerable. In general, lonely people have fewer family members with whom they can talk. In times of crisis, such as bereavement, they are more likely than most people to need support from social services or from their doctors. The most common cause of loneliness is thought to be the death of close friends or relatives. Loneliness thus arises because of lack of close social contact. It means that the individual lacks special relationships or one special relationship which enables her to share important experiences. Such communication helps someone to judge his or her own value as well as evaluating things that happen to them. When there is nobody to talk with the person cannot judge these values and events in the same way. Many lonely people come to feel that they are of no value to anyone, and this inhibits them from seeking to reduce their isolation. I will return to these points very shortly.

What implications might this brief discussion have for Mrs Smith's sense of personal identity? To put it briefly, it seems to me that sociological concepts of the person and interpersonal relationships and psycho-dynamic approaches to emotion and subjective experience are potentially helpful. A number of related sociological perspectives emphasise the interaction between individual and social situations and are referred to as interactionist. They focus on small-scale interaction rather than on society as a whole and question the notion of human action in terms of simple responses or reactions to the social system. These perspectives are sometimes referred to as phenomenological because of their emphasis on the individual's views and interpretations of social reality. The social world is defined by individuals' subjective experiences. These approaches have been summarised by the sentence: if men define situations as real they are real in their consequences (Thomas, 1966). They emphasise their focus on the processes by which members of society define their circumstances and respective identities. Starting from the assumption that experience is meaningful to those involved, it follows that understanding it involves interpreting the meanings individuals give to their experience.

In contemporary society, close relationships, marriage being a striking example, have a primary place in validating personal identity. The macro-social world may give rise to feelings of anxiety and loneliness, as we found in Mrs Smith's experience. This world may send conflicting messages to the individual in communicating apparently contradictory injunctions to individuals to mourn those they have loved, but not to allow their grief to intrude and make other people uncomfortable. Mrs Smith still needed people to talk to but 'they did not want to know'.

Berger and Kellner (1970) indicate that the individual and her partner act on her social reality which, in a reciprocal exchange, then acts back on her, so producing a new and unique social world. They suggest that a common history is developed for the people involved so that marriage means acquiring new roles, the creation of a new social world and the development of identity. In trying to construct another role as widow, Mrs Smith was probably seen by the social worker to face considerable problems in realising that she must make a new life for herself without the partner whom she felt had been part of her self. It seems reasonable to say that social work help for individuals should be based on an understanding of the existential needs and social situations of the people involved and this can be furthered by understanding the ways in which meaningful relationships develop.

Smith (1975) points out that the individual's relation to the social world is circumscribed by the behaviour which comprises a pattern of roles. But roles are not provided in a simple way by social systems, and in Mrs Smith's case it seems that one of her 'problems' is to discover how she will assume the role of widow. On the evidence available one can speculate about how far the loss of her husband contributed to Mrs Smith feeling a lack of meaning in her life. If her personal identity depends to a large degree on confirmation through interaction with her husband, has this loss upset the stability of her social world? The social worker seems to think that it has. Individuals do not enact their roles as if they are reading off a script containing explicit directions about how to behave. Roles are sometimes vague and ambiguous, and people therefore have considerable room for creativity, improvisation and negotiation. Roles provide guidelines for behaviour – not blueprints. In relationships like marriage, for example, people have only general ideas about the roles of husband and wife. Their definitions of wife, husband and a marital relationship will be negotiated in the course of time. Every individual needs the ongoing validation of her world, and this includes her identity, and of her place in the world. This validation goes on in interaction with significant others. Individuals also seem to need a private sphere in which to construct a mini-society of their own if wider society is anonymous and alien. Family members, for example, constitute just such a discrete mini-society. In seeking validation of her identity from others, the individual seeks affirmation of her 'self'.

The material presented here invites consideration of a range of factors which may have influenced the social worker and Mrs Smith. I would like to refer briefly to the possible influence of the social services organisation. What follows is based on discussions with members of the intake team, including the team leader, and the social worker who interviewed Mrs Smith. In common with other social services departments the ethos of the work of this intake team tended to be to deal with the problem presented and then close the case. In conducting initial interviews social workers commonly tried to control the conversation by focusing on topics they saw as being related to the presenting request and giving less attention to matters which could not be so defined or easily categorised. They were quite likely to keep the focus on the applicant's request or the problem as given at referral and not consider other problems. In another study of intake work it was found that most of the social workers interviewed did not investigate problems other than the immediate ones presented by the applicant. It was suggested that even where social workers became aware of other problems they might blind themselves to their full importance and make conscious efforts to deal only with the presenting problem (Prodgers, 1979).

From my discussions with the social workers in the intake team it was apparent that they felt under pressure from the department to try to fit the people and situations that confronted them into certain categories. They saw this as helping them to define the kinds of intervention that might be appropriate and to assess the degree of priority to give each new referral. It helped them to identify cases as easy or difficult, and as potentially short-term or long-term. The intake team as a whole, including the senior social worker, saw their service to clients as primarily problem focused. They were not expected to develop close relationships with clients. They saw their work as accepting a referral (or directing inappropriate applicants elsewhere) and working on specific problems with clients, for example, helping them to negotiate with the Department of Health and Social Security helping them to reach decisions about accepting day or residential care, or holding a series of interviews about family problems. They aimed to close cases as quickly as possible and any cases remaining open after three months, following review, were transferred to long-term workers. The social worker's interview with Mrs Smith was discussed with the intake team leader with her permission. The team leader clearly thought that the social worker should have accepted the definition of the referral as it was given by the doctor who referred Mrs Smith. In other words, the social worker should have restricted her focus to the request for registration as a disabled person. The social worker, in his opinion, should not have attempted to explore how Mrs Smith herself perceived her situation. The team leader thus defined the reality of the situation very differently. (I should add that at a later date he told me that he had changed his mind – he thought he had been mistaken and overly censorious.) Clearly defined tasks and limited time involvement are generally accepted as significant features of intake work. When social workers and clients are able to agree explicitly about the problems to be dealt with and the tasks are clear, then these cases are most likely to be given high priority. Where problems are less well defined or social workers and clients do not agree about them, these cases will often be given lower priority. It may then be expected that people experiencing loneliness and coping with bereavement would be regarded as having lower priority by most intake teams.

Although it is an oversimplification to suggest that workers in intake teams have either a 'bureacratic' or a 'treatment' orientation to their work, these two general types are of some use. They provide a basis for studying the relationship between social workers' actions and their employing organisations if they are regarded as positions on a continuum. Social workers do not hold to a single orientation and they play different roles at different times. I found that this was the case with Mrs Smith's social worker as well as other members of the intake team. It seems that intake workers have to find ways of coping with conflicts between what they see as their 'professional' as distinct from their 'bureaucratic' tasks. It seems that they are caught between looking for innovative and individual solutions and routine bureaucratic ones. The case of Mrs Smith and the social worker thus provides a vivid illustration of the tensions which can exist when treatment orientated social workers operate in bureaucratically organised agencies. The team leader very vehemently declared that the social worker should not have given time to discussing matters apart from the application for registration as disabled. His view was that the worker should not have envisaged extended contact with Mrs Smith and that she was wrong to consider giving her so much time.

Using the evidence of tape-recorded excerpts I have tried to indicate some aspects of how the social worker seemed to 'construct' the reality of Mrs Smith's situation and tried to understand it 'through her eyes'. Another approach would have been to try to understand Mrs Smith's own reality, but I did not interview her myself. I have discussed some questions about the communication of what subjective experience means to another person, a social worker in this instance. Questions have also been raised about social workers' frames of reference for interpreting the client's meanings and the relationship between these and decisions about possible intervention. If you accept the kind of interpretation I first gave of the interview with Mrs Smith, you would be likely to take no further action. This kind of interpretation can be accepted easily if some verbal and non-verbal cues are rejected. If, however, the social worker is sensitive and open to the client's words and actions, as this social worker appeared to be, a very different picture may emerge. It is one which involves attempting to understand less tangible aspects of behaviour and experience like loneliness, self-esteem, personal identity and depression. It involves living with the uncertainty and anxiety which inevitably accompany reflection and self-discovery. I suggest that further work could be of value on these topics which are of common interest to sociologists and psycho-therapists. Both may contribute to thinking about social work practice.

The attempt to understand how Mrs Smith, the social worker, the team leader and I tried to make sense of her situation clearly involved more than describing subjective experiences. The interplay between these subjective experiences and the social context, particularly the social service organisation, has to be borne in mind. It has only been possible to mention some of the influences and constraints involved in Mrs Smith's referral. But we have confronted questions about how priorities are defined and how such isues may be affected by the values and ideologies of social workers and social services departments. I think that they give us grounds to give further attention to clients' experiences of initial interviews and the responsibilities of intake workers.

Conclusion

We have seen that although it has limitations, systems theory is of help to social workers in focusing on the interaction between individuals and their environment. The family may be thought of as a system made up of people who interact with each other in some characteristic ways; whether social workers approach family units as a whole or decide to work mainly with family sub-systems depends on who they think is mainly involved or affected by problems or pressures within or outside the family. The nature of the problems affects this decision. Problems of financial management, sexual relationships, or other private concerns of the adults are probably best dealt with by the adults rather than younger family members. It might be undesirable to expose them to some of the revelations of adults about their sex lives, threats to their self-esteem, their ill health or their employment problems. This is not to suggest that they should never take a part in discussions of this nature, since sometimes they could and should be involved. What is suggested is that it is important to consider the vulnerability of people who may be concerned. The approach used also depends on their capacity to deal with problems, which is affected by the physical and emotional resources of family members. The short- or long-term goals of intervention are also important. The concerns of the family group may take priority over individual problems and lead to work with the family as a whole or with parts of a family. This chapter has been aimed at illustrating some ways in which sociology can help to clarify processes leading to stresses and crises associated with family disorganisation, and individual and group approaches in social work intervention. A number of issues mentioned here in working with families also arise in working with non-family groups.

Social work with families and individuals and other groups is crucially dependent on communication. We noted that it cannot be assumed that clients and social workers will have similar expectations of the interview and each other. When they have incongruent perceptions of each others' roles there will be obstacles to communication between them. If they are to understand and help to modify obstacles to communication, social workers need to be informed about cultural and class differences. It needs to be recognised, however, that the satisfaction of clients with social work service, for example in the case of ethnic minorities, depends on more than securing improved communication. Social workers need to guard against dismissing problems merely as signs of cultural differences and saying that they should simply be tolerated out of respect for a different culture. They also need to guard against evading responsibility by stressing the self-help traditions of other cultures. Sociological findings can also help to alert social workers to the dangers of making stereotyped generalisations about cultures and social classes. The terms 'working class' and 'middle class' do not in reality apply to homogeneous groups in this country today. Some attitudes and aspirations formerly described as 'middle class' are found among people described as 'working class'. Similarly, some behaviour called 'middle class' probably only applies to certain business and professional people. There is considerable overlapping in the life styles of social classes, which social workers need to bear in mind in their work with applicants for help.

The urgent necessity for social workers to understand social and cultural influences on behaviour and family life has been emphasised in work with people from different ethnic groups. Sociological understanding of family problems and findings about family disorganisation and violence provides indications about potentially helpful forms of intervention. Interactionist perspectives have been contrasted with other approaches and they have been illustrated through the use of tape recordings of interviews between a social worker and a client and subsequent discussion of the interview with the social worker. This material itself suggests a different way of thinking about practice and the kinds of influences which affect clients and social workers, and the social service organisation in particular. The illustration cannot be regarded as a model of this sociological approach, but I think that it suggests its considerable potential and shows that positive and constructive ideas can be generated about different views of a person's situation.

5

The Social Context of Social Work Practice

Social work and uncertainty

The practice of social work is very difficult to define. Social work, unlike medicine for example, is not a clearly defined technical profession based on scientific knowledge directly applied in practice. Social work practice is beset by uncertainties about the nature and relevance of much information and about theories relating particularly to individual welfare and community development in a complicated society. It is misleading to refer to *the* social work task because social workers have many tasks, and it is not clear that social work can be identified as an activity, as teaching or nursing can. In practice social workers have a number of functions in the social services, and they deal with various problems which are experienced by different kinds of individuals and groups. Society (including many social groups from the legislature, the judiciary, and groups of citizens representing various interests) expects social workers to be both caring and controlling, but there are different views about the weighting to be given to the two in different situations. In addition, there are sometimes conflicting ideas about social workers as omnipotent on the one hand and as not possessing any special expertise on the other.

Social work and social control

Social workers act as agents of social control. They are involved in the compulsory admission to hospital or guardianship of people suffering from mental disorders, and it is recognised that the social worker's primary professional contribution here is the assessment of community-based alternatives to hospital care. Account has to be taken of the family, cultural and social context of the person who is thought to need help. The social worker is responsible for maintaining independence and impartiality when assessing patients' needs and the care and support which should be provided in the community. The social worker's functions relate principally to matters affecting the liberty of the individual patient. Social workers are required by law to investigate possible violence or harm to children by their parents, and to undertake surveillance of families after these alleged incidents have come to their notice. They are finally responsible for deciding whether a case of non-accidental injury should be taken to court or whether a child in care may go home on trial. These decisions are nearly always made in consultation with other people, including nurses, doctors, teachers and the police. Procedures have been developed to enable information to be collected and shared in order that decisions will be made on the basis of detailed consideration. The difficulties and dilemmas for social workers arising from the dual functions of social caring and control are not at all easy, although they are an intrinsic feature of social work practice. It has been said that if it is part of the social worker's function to help people adjust to the expectations of the society in which they live, it is equally part of their function to criticise these expectations, describing some as unrealistic or irrational and others as unethical. Society has no business to expect social workers to further a one-sided process of adaptation, all the change being demanded of the clients and none at all in social expectations. On the contrary, society must expect the social work profession to derive from its experience of working with clients, understandings about society's responsibility for the attitudes and behaviour which it finds damaging or inconvenient. And it must expect to be told by social workers that their role is to be involved in social as well as individual change: it is not that of engineering a passive conformity to unacceptable social norms. In a pluralistic rather than a consensus society there are many different perspectives on the working of the social structure and social problems and how to deal with them. These different views are reflected in conflicting and inconsistent attitudes towards the range of tasks social workers perform. Concern with human problems of living calls for attention both to people and to the social circumstances in which they live. The balance between these two aspects of intervention may vary considerably depending, for example, on the influence of factors such as understanding of the nature and causes of these problems, and prevailing social values. The relative emphasis given to the internal and external aspects of human problems fluctuates; social work is open to such changes and not all these changing fashions in practice are necessarily logical or consistent.

Sociology and the nuances of social work practice

An analysis of occupations aptly shows how sociological examination can sensitise us to the nuances of social work practice. It shows how practice is multi-faceted and needs to be understood as being about many things, each based on different concepts and different kinds of knowledge (Howe, 1980). Seen as a role job, social work can be understood in relation to the rights, duties and responsibilities involved. Social work practice is socially sanctioned and social workers as operating in an institutional framework which requires them to be interested in the actions of other members of the community. Given the right to intervene, they necessarily have rights and responsibilities; and other citizens know that they legitimately perform certain functions, and have preconceived ideas about what they can expect from social workers. Many clients see social workers as officials employed to check up on needy old people and to make sure that children are properly cared for. A considerable part of social workers' relationships with their clients can be understood by both groups as a set of legally defined rights, either in terms of what clients may expect or of what social workers may do. The nature of much of its involvement with adult offenders, children and adolescents and handicapped and mentally disordered people is in line with such a description. For some people social work is primarily recognisable because of the skills which are used. These range from knowing and handling the environment and its resources to knowing about and handling people. Claims have been made about skills in human relationships. But it is hard to understand the job just in terms of some of the skills many workers say they possess. For some social workers the idea of technique has come to be dominant, and the reasons for their employment seem to have been forgotten.

Much emphasis has been placed on social work being a job which is recognisable essentially because of the skills its practitioners use. Supposing that skills in inter-personal relationships can be recognised in the first place, this may not lead observers to conclude that what they are seeing is social work rather than the practice of psychiatry or health visiting. The claim to have skills and expertise may not be recognised by other people: if they do not accept that certain skills exist they will not see the skill job being offered. The techniques used in social work are relatively simple and, as Sainsbury (1982) points out, some would challenge the term 'techniques' because they are so simple. In social work, techniques may be superseded because they are considered in some way (morally, economically, organisationally or politically) inappropriate, or do not 'feel right'. Disputes about the validity of techniques owe more to the preferences and interests of the disputants than to systematic research. Sometimes information may be helpful in understanding what is going on but not of use in developing the ability to do something. Making judgements and choices may help in practising skills. Occupations are also analysed by reference to their aims. There are different kinds of aims in social work and those suggested as intrinsic to its practice seem to vary according to the values held by individuals. Examples of intrinsic aims include promoting the welfare of and upholding respect for the individual as client, and being concerned for the well-being of the whole community. According to this argument social work may involve dealing with social and economic circumstances affecting individuals, or it is a job concerned with the welfare of people with problems in coping with life in a complex society, and aims to help them to improve their functioning. Choosing between these features of the job can be thought of as matters of personal values or tastes, and such choices involve applying different kinds of knowledge and using different skills. Casework or counselling and community work can be regarded as more than two different methods of working: they differ in terms of their assumptions, theories and practices. They sometimes have different ways of seeing people in society. It may not be necessary (even if it is conceivable) to group all of the complexity of views of social realities or to fit them into one particular theoretical system in order to intervene in social situations. Social work has been seduced into looking for 'knowledge of social reality' (rather than understanding multiple perspectives) and seeking to exercise control and to manipulate systems and individuals. In making grandiose and pretentious claims the results have inevitably been disappointing. These issues will be taken up again shortly.

Social work practice in context

Our understanding of contemporary social work practice may be increased if we study the political, social and historical context. It seems self-evident that practice is related to the society of which it is a part, and its functions or operations depend on the social structure and are affected by social change. In being involved with people and their social situations, social work is exposed to external influences and various interpretations and views of its nature. In recent years social workers have been given increasing responsibility and power in containing, controlling and alleviating many major social problems. Its development has clearly been linked with the recognition by the state of the desirability of providing for deviant, sick, disabled and disadvantaged people and for children and elderly people requiring care. Different interpretations of such developments help indicate the ways sociological understanding may show how practice itself has been influenced by theory, ideology and oranisational and institutional pressures. They also show how practice responds and reacts to different social policies, themselves influenced by theories and ideologies. Clearly these relationships are not easily understood, and the situation is further complicated, as we will see, because different theoretical approaches have been used at different times, and have also been seen as more relevant to particular social problems and aspects of social life. It will be helpful to illustrate part of this complexity with an historical note about the development of social work.

For some time consensus theories have been taken for granted by most social workers as underpinning practice which helps to reduce strains or conflicts in society, in particular by seeking to achieve a balance between the interests of the individual and the community. It is assumed that there is a basic shared system of values, and even though differences between social classes are acknowledged, 'deviants' are encouraged to conform to the communal value system. From this point of view social work is an agency of control which may facilitate some changes while mainly contributing to the maintenance of social order. Casework, particularly in the United States, developed while function-alist sociologists were dominant and during a period when there were serious problems of poverty and unemployment in the United States and Britain. At the time the two societies were relatively stable and the authority of establishment figures was not seriously challenged. Developments in the United States influenced social work in Britain. In particular the idea that unemployment, crime, homelessness and poverty were caused by individual pathology or inadequacy apparent-ly dominated the thinking of social workers. There was a growth in welfare services during the long economic boom following World War II. In the post-war period attempts to restore conservative social norms were reinforced by ideas about the supposed dangers of maternal deprivation. There was greater emphasis on the importance of 'normal' family life, and there was pressure for women to return from war work to running the home and to revert to the traditional roles of housewives and mothers. The 1950s was a period when there was little to challenge social casework, although there was some intellectual criticism of its dominance at the end of the decade. In this country the social work elite developed the application of psychology to casework, and the influence of these ideas increased as social work education expanded following the Younghusband Report (1959). Casework was used as a unifying ideology, and this may have contributed to further the formation of a unified profession. Strong support for casework was seen in research which pointed to the dangers of bad practice in the institutional care of children. Impersonal residential institutions meant that young children were unable to form continuing close relationships with familiar adults so that, although physical needs were met, the developing child was emotionally damaged. Bowlby first suggested that a number of social problems (criminal behaviour, mental disorder and juvenile delinquency) were in many cases the result of broken homes and deprivation of maternal care. Although Bowlby's ideas were modified by later research their initial impact had important effects on social work. A positive result of Bowlby's work was to increase interest in the provision of more humane institutions for children, thus reinforcing the view that the conservative Poor Law ideology was outdated. It led eventually to acceptance of the view that institutionalisation could also lead to psychological and physical deterioration of adults living in homes for the elderly, in mental hospitals and prisons. This helped support criticisms of institutional care and the promotion of the idea of 'community care' as an alternative (Barton, 1976).

This general position and the over-ambitious claims made by caseworkers were challenged in 1959 when Wootton wrote that social workers had failed to emancipate themselves from a mystical view of the 'casework process' and the 'relationship'. They were steeped in the mysteries of Freudianism, and these trends had deflected attention away from the problems created by 'evil environments'. She hoped for radical changes in attitude and also hoped that putting the 'social' back into social work implied a relaxation of the popular attempts to imitate psycho-analysis and a realisation of such facts as that families live among neighbours and not in a vacuum, that people spend a high proportion of their time at work, and that they are affected by what happens outside their homes as well as by their domestic relationships. Wootton, among others, clearly perceived the value of sociological perspectives, even if her condemnation of psychology could appear to be intemperate. In the 1960s a minority of social workers actively challenged the establishment by drawing attention to the problems of poor housing, poverty and unemployment. Social workers in general were reluctant to challenge the *status quo*. This may have been due in large part to the search for professional status: social work's strong interests in the existing order may have caused it to compromise. During the depression in the USA, for example, social workers advocated radical reforms, but they seemed always to assume that there should be no radical changes in the economic and social systems. The application of conflict theories leads to a view of social work practice in the context of conflicting class interests. Social work is seen as not being aimed at the maintenance of stability and order, but as acting on behalf of particular class interests by working alongside underprivileged people.

From the 1950s onwards there was a movement inspired by conservative practitioners and academics who were concerned to unify social work as a profession, and the setting up of generic training during this period reflected the reaction against the existing specialisms. Probation officers played a leading part in this movement, but did not join the British Association of Social Workers because of their fears about the possible consequences of re-organisation of the social services, and they became suspicious about genericism. In 1968 the Seebohm Committee was set up to consider the managerial and organisatonal divisions of local authority child care and welfare departments, and urged that unified departments of social service should be created. When the new departments came into existence in 1970 they represented the culmination of post-war developments. They involved a partnership between social work, with its aspirations to be a unified profession, and the managerial requirements of local authorities and the state. The Seebohm Committee recommended that the unified social services departments should provide a family-focused service directed to the well-being of the whole community and not only of social casualties. However, the new departments became responsible for administering a range of means-tested benefits and their clients were mainly the most disadvantaged individuals, families and groups in the community. Their image was that of an agency which catered for 'social casualties' and in which considered emphasis was placed on a hierarchical system of managerial control and bureaucratic co-ordination. These developments, with the increases in statutory requirements, seem to have powerfully affected the work roles and practices of social workers. Within the social, economic and political conditions of a state bureaucracy, professional tensions became sharpened and intensified, particularly whether social workers' primary loyalties were towards clients or to society. Social workers became disillusioned and found that much of the traditional social work 'knowledge' failed to cope with the new problems of clients and social workers.

In a climate of thought which saw separate fields of practice like child care, medical social work and probation, and supposedly different 'methods' of intervention like casework, groupwork and community work, as not being distinct and separate but as parts of a whole, there were attempts to provide unified concepts for social work practice. I will be discussing this subject in more detail, but we can note that the so-called integrated or unitary approach was first developed in the USA. It is based on the idea that instead of seeing themselves as practitioners of casework (or counselling), groupwork or community work, social workers should see themselves as change agents who intervene at different levels at different times, with individuals, groups or organisations, to effect change. Social work practice seemed to be based on an approach which emphasised consensual views of social reality. This systems approach was enthusiastically embraced, particularly by academics but also by some practitioners. It has advantages in underlining the relationship between individuals and their social situations, but it is open to question whether it has added to existing practice. The problem seems to be that at any given time social work practice is specific. It is concerned with understanding a particular situation confronting a certain client and social worker in a particular organisation. You cannot understand this situation by discovering a single general theory, if one exists, nor is there a single generic principle which can be used to handle the situation.

Communities and social work

The Seebohm Report recommended that social services should be community-based, and described community by saying that it implied the existence of a network of reciprocal relationships, which, among other things, ensure mutual aid and give those who experience it a sense of well-being. The Barclay Report (1982) said that an important feature of community is the capacity of the people within it to mobilise individual and collective responses to adversity. The sum of helping (and, when need be, controlling) resources available to people in adversity, whether provided informally by community networks or formally by public services, was referred to as social care. The Barclay Committee advocated a community approach to social work which would seek a closer working partnership between citizens and the personal social services. The approach could not be fully implemented in only one part of the social services: housing, health and education services were equally or more important. Essentially, community social work would involve the development of flexible decentralised organisations based on a plan for social care which took full account of informal care, and mobilised voluntary and statutory provision. The focus of social work changed from the individual, seen in sharp relief against a rather hazy social background, to seeing people as members of families. Community social work required the widening of the circle of vision to include people who formed or might form the individual's social network. Social workers needed to consider the various people with whom the individual was in touch, to focus on the actual or potential links which existed or could be fostered between people in a geographical area, hospital or residential home, and to bear in mind communities of interest which develop between people who sometimes share concerns because they suffer from the same social problems. Community social work implies a focus on individuals and families in the context of all the networks of which they do, or might, form a part. This work may be based on geographical locality (centred on patch teams, social workers in hospital or attached to general practices or schools) or on shared concern (centred on specialist teams at area level or multi-disciplinary teams serving a wider population). It requires understanding of the interactions of people in groups and communities, and a capacity to negotiate and to bring people together to enable networks to grow. A minority view questioned what these ideas implied. Reservations about community- and neighbourhood-based social services included the view that insufficient attention may have been given to the capacity of local communities to provide informal care. The public social services developed because local communities were incapable of meeting the kind of personal needs which arise in complex industrial societies. Under the Poor Law, the most localised system of social service, it was its localised (parochial) nature which added the painful experience of stigma among recipients of poor relief. In the community-based models of social work the most vulnerable, disadvantaged and stigmatised clients could be at greatest risk, as they give greatest offence to local norms of behaviour and were often rejected by their local communities.

The Barclay Report dealt with skills and methods in social work practice in a short chapter, and made a helpful distinction between practical knowledge which can be used and made available to clients, and knowledge about how people behave. It said that the skills required by social workers need to be based on knowledge or information for immediate use and knowledge that provides insight into the behaviour of people, organisations and societies and how that behaviour might change. Information for immediate use includes knowledge of the agency and the area in which the social worker works and the resources (people, organisations, services and materials) available there. Knowledge that provides insight into behaviour includes understanding how societies, cultures and organisations function with particular reference to structures of social control, the forces generating social change and the ways in which control and change are affected by different political beliefs, and understanding of family and community relationships, and how they differ in different cultures. The social worker needs to understand that all such knowledge rests on evidence that can be differently interpreted from different perspectives, and that moral, philosophical and political assumptions underlie formulations of theory. Social workers have to choose among courses of action knowing that no one course of action can be guaranteed as infallible, and that there are different views among social workers about values. One writer at least has seen this as a strength of social work. Values cannot be discussed in isolation from the pressures of specific situations and role perspectives since the same people may hold different (or even incompatible) values in different circumstances. They may promote or demote a specific value in relation to changing perceptions of their roles and the roles of other people. Values like 'self-determination' may sound good in college or in meetings but may look sick in the context of some aspects of practice (Sainsbury, 1982).

Ways in which sociologists analyse values are discussed in the course of this book. For the present we need to observe that values cannot be discussed in isolation from knowledge and skills. Awareness of expertise in a field of knowledge leads the individual to stress the relative importance of those aspects of a situation in which this knowledge or skill may be exercised. The individual's values influence what he or she sees as the 'facts' of a situation and what is seen as 'relevant' knowledge. You cannot discuss the knowledge base of social work without paying attention to its application as skill and to the values implicit in the selection of knowledge. You cannot discuss the teaching of practice skills without considering their legitimisation in both theoretical and moral terms. A value system for social work cannot be formulated without considering the social circumstances and role contexts in which values are expressed.

Conclusion

Most of the topics discussed in this chapter, as elsewhere in the book, are highly controversial. We may have different ideas about what the aims of social work should or could be, but it is evident that social workers operate at various levels in the social structure. A major feature of social work practice is the social worker's own self and position. The social worker's self cannot be ignored when the quality of social work practice is considered. Social workers have to think about their use of their selves in a variety of contexts, and about their social positions and the different roles they play. Much has been written about interviewing as a major activity in social work which, we have seen, draws on a range of techniques and theories. This aspect of social work may be thought of as the context of two people, and it may well extend to other people as well.

Group dynamics have been regarded as central to social work practice. In working with individuals, as I have just indicated, it may well be very important that various groups such as work, neighbourhood and family should be considered. In neighbourhood or community projects the views of different groups have to be taken into account. These included formal bodies such as statutory agencies, local council members, voluntary groups, and informal groups based, for example, on schools, pubs, churches and shops. The fourth context of social work practice is organisational. Two features which are usually recognised are: (a) the goals of the organisation, its powers and methods of working, and its systems and sub-systems of communication and decision-making; and (b) the positions in the organisation occupied by social worker and clients.

Some of the reasons why social work practice is difficult to define and suggestions about sociology's contribution to examination of the problems have been outlined. It has been stressed that social work has to be seen as a product of the society in which it functions, and is affected both by the social and individual problems occurring in society and by the attitudes affecting the response to these problems. Social control is a feature of social work and the term, of course, denotes the ways in which people are constrained in their behaviour by the norms of groups, organisations or communities of which they are members. For functionalists or consensus theorists, social control involves acceptance of values which it is supposed all members of society accept. These shared values underlie social stability or equilibrium, and social control is the complex of forces which makes equilibrium or facilitates its restoration. By accepting a model of society as a social system based on a fundamental consensus about underlying social values, one social work task is that of helping to pass on these accepted values to individuals and groups whose socialisation has been 'deficient'. Social work clients can then be regarded as being social failures, maladjusted or deviant. To suggest that the function of social work is solely social control is, of course, an oversimplification. For example, care and control are performed through social agencies but, in addition, they have functions to perform in relation to social change, and in supposedly supporting other social institutions like the family if they are to adapt to social changes which occur in modern society.

The relationship between society and social work is extremely complex. The problems presented to social workers are often of concern to the community, and the social agency is then seen as one way in which the community seeks to promote conformity on the part of clients and, in this sense, has social control functions. By its nature, the social agency is normative and judgemental, and the majority of social workers in the United Kingdom work in statutory agencies with powers and duties relating to the care of children and elderly and handicapped people. An examination of social workers' roles, skills and aims has implications for the kinds of knowledge to be applied in different forms of practice. Studying the development of social work practice throws some light on contemporary issues of this kind.

6

Social Work Practice: Groups and Organisations

Working with groups

A wide variety of situations may call for the application of group work ideas. Family interviews, meeting with three or more people in a waiting room or in the street, at school or at work, tenants or neighbourhood groups, recreational activity groups, social clubs and many others constitute likely settings. They all involve interaction between individuals. A social worker involved in these situations will need to understand and use the exchanges between people rather than just his or her own relationship with each of them individually.

The word 'group' is a way of summarising and expressing a very wide and complicated range of human experiences and phenomena. It is used by Davies (1975) to refer to a gathering of three or more people; who may, but who may not, expect to go one meeting permanently. In it direct person-to-person exchanges (verbal or non-verbal) between each individual are at least possible and there exists or is possible among these individuals some common interests or purposes, some sense of identity and some mutual acceptance of interdependence. This practical definition is necessarily flexible: it allows for groups of various sizes, for single or more frequent meetings, and for more or less structured and planned proceedings. It is important for practical purposes to underline the actual or potential size, the key question for social workers being whether gatherings are useable.

Arguments arise about how many people constitute a

group and when a small group ceases to be small and becomes large. They also arise about the physical properties of a group. Must all individuals be in the same place at the same time for the group to be said to exist? Or does the group continue to exist when its members are geographically dispersed? How often and for how long do people need to be in contact to be thought of as a group? Does a group exist if outsiders call a gathering a group, or must members themselves have a subjective sense of belonging together? All of these issues are relevant to group work practice. Disciplined work with groups requires understanding of how and why individuals sense their involvement with others and why they are willing to commit themselves to them. Many social workers would see groups as:

(a) centres for practical activity
(b) gatherings of a number of people who meet regularly to work on the same or similar tasks
(c) a developing organism composed of interacting and independent individuals.

Often those who work with groups see them as primarily places where quite practical tasks are tackled. The apparent raison d'être of groups is what they do.

Group work and the community

The importance of having some understanding of the social background of clients and families has been emphasised in social casework. Using work with pre-delinquent or delinquent youth as one illustration, I now want to consider the importance of the community in relation to group work. Young people may cause problems for other residents in their neighbourhoods. Communal tensions of many kinds often develop out of proportion to the incidents which trigger them initially. In the case of adolescents they may result in demands that particular teenagers or children should be removed from the community and taken into care. As part of their task, intermediate treatment workers may be expected to provide supervision and control to some troublesome youngsters and to play the role of intermediary between them and others in the locality. Some localities may predispose young people towards trouble. It may be that residents are not particularly concerned about delinquent behaviour. It may be that children are unsupervised and have poor recreation facilities so that there is little to divert them from delinquency. One task for intermediate treatment workers could be to press for increased community facilities and to look for ways to make the impact of the neighbourhood on adolescents more positive. The client's neighbourhood should be taken into account in planning group work since local resources can be mobilised to help. Take intermediate treatment as an example. It seems that social workers and others think of the quality of parental care an individual received from his parents and the influence of friends as important in predisposition to delinquency. Next they see neighbourhood facilities or lack of them, and the attitudes of people in the neighbourhood, as important. In aiming to keep young people out of trouble, intermediate treatment projects are thought of as compensating for lack of neighbourhood facilities and relieving boredom. The attitudes of local residents to adolescents may become more positive if they can be shown that those perceived as troublesome and selfish also have the potential to be helpful and constructive. It follows that intermediate treatment programmes should be planned to be relevant to life in the individual's neighbourhood.

Social services and neighbourhood teams

Methods of neighbourhood work and team work recognise the advantages of teams pooling their experience of clients and acting co-operatively to find solutions. Research on work groups and how they function has been reviewed by Adamson (1983), who explores sources of stress and how more effective groups might develop. It has been shown that group performance rests on having appropriate styles of leadership – 'appropriate' meaning that which matches the characteristics of the group, the task to be carried out and the power of the leader. The idea of appropriate leadership means that at each phase different inputs are required. A nurturing style of leadership would be appropriate at the initial, formative stage of a new group, whereas an energising style would subsequently become the appropriate leadership input (Randall and Southgate, 1981). In the early stages of organisational life, doctrinal loyalty, aggressiveness and enthusiasm, and personal charismatic qualities are required. Later, quieter, more controlled, routinised administrative skills are needed. Research challenges the idea that leadership problems can be solved by choosing individuals with certain personal characterisitics to take leadership roles. It seems that work groups operate effectively when they enable a wide range of people to contribute. Work groups with inappropriate and unskilled leadership will be ineffective and dull at best. At worst, they will be hostile and destructive for their members.

There seem to be three basic principles for the management of organisational change. The process of reform always encourages conflict. People confronted with change need the chance to react and to try to verbalise their mixed feelings about it. Second, the process must respect the autonomy of different kinds of experience. Third, time and patience are needed because conflicts involve the accommodation of diverse interests. Team building is widely used in the promotion of organisational change, and is based on a collaborative or action research approach. The key phases of this approach are information gathering, diagnosis of problems, feedback to the work group, discussion and action planning, and action. The structural facilitation of change involves creating learning systems and communication networks, which are more important than the authority structure. Put in another way, vertical bureaucracies are poor learning systems as they are inevitably subject to culture lag. Structures are needed which are more open to change and learning. They should be horizontal rather than hierarchical (Schon, 1971).

The leader needs to be aware of the team's dynamics as a working group, and should facilitate team members' participation in agreeing and implementing decisions so that they will be committed to acting on them. Team meetings provide the opportunity for open discussions in which everyone is encouraged to contribute, and they can cover a range of topics, including work allocation, consultations and conferences on case work and group work, and issues internal or external to the organisation. The team can be an important vehicle of professional development in which members can share skills and learn from each other's knowledge and experience. For this to happen, teams and team leaders will need to bear in mind the composition of the team when selecting new members – the balance of experienced and inexperienced staff and of people whose skills complement each other, as well as the age and sex composition of the group and the compatibility of their personalities. Team leaders cannot be expected to have detailed knowledge of all the work their teams cover, but they should have th capacity to identify the roles of members and to foster their strengths so that they are used for the benefit of the whole group. It is important to remember that team members welcome directiveness as well as constructive criticism and control from their leaders (Stevenson and Parsloe, 1979).

Control and communication in social services

While it is supposed to be a non-bureaucratic type of control, social work supervision is often used to enforce the administrative requirements of the bureaucratic organisation (social services departments in particular), such as meeting reporting deadlines, while avoiding too great an undermining of the professional's self-image. The supervisor works on the assumption that the junior social worker's non-conformity to agency requirements is a function of the junior's lack of awareness which only the supervisor or other senior staff understand. The supervisor emphasises the educational nature of his role and plays down his image of bureaucrat. Conflict can be avoided through the professional's way of adapting to work originating in the bureaucratic aspects of the organisation. Administrative tasks can be described in terms of professional practice. For example, legal requirements about the frequency of visits can be thought of in terms of service to the client. This may not be possible: the ability to accept authority may then be regarded as an indication of professional self-discipline. A third way is to place organisational rules which appear contrary to the clients' interests in the context of a theory justifying them in terms of client welfare. As the Hawthorne studies showed, patterns of activity in organisations cannot be explained solely in terms of the formal patterns of interaction. Far from being necessary in large organisations, bureaucracies create as many problems as they solve. Look, for example, at the effect of a formal bureacratic structure on the flow of communication. Most organisations which are formally bureaucratic only work because they have an informal organisation.

Although there is a formal hierarchy of authority in social work organisations, power is dispersed to a very limited extent in that front-line members have to use their initiative and this sometimes includes deciding when to refer to superiors. The official goals of these organisations are stated in general terms only and they are implemented by front-line staff. Control over general policy is exercised by those at the centre, as they have responsibility for standards of performance in executing policy. This control is exercised to a great degree through the structure of communication. By requiring that copies of letters and reports, and that regular statistical and other information, for example, is sent to the divisional office and headquarters they may attempt to ensure a free flow of upward communication. They can limit access to information which the organisation receives from other organisations and information which are collated internally. This confers power on senior management in several ways, and in local authorities, for example, this includes the possibility of influencing elected representatives. Other methods of control include the appointment and deployment of field and residential staff and devising ways of monitoring the work of area teams and residential homes, and promoting policy changes. The advantages of bureaucracy are not always fully acknowledged. They include precision and speed in making some decisions, impartiality and some public accountability, as well as support and supervision by more experienced workers. Evidence about the effects of bureaucracy sometimes seems to be conflicting. It has been found that staff employed in large-scale bureaucratic organisations were more open-minded, self-directed, flexible and receptive to change in their attitudes than staff in smaller, less formal organisations. This was associated with the more protected position of staff in bureaucracies and the more clearly defined authority over them.

Some researchers regard hierarchical forms of organisation as being destructive of positive human relationships and point to various modifications of hierarchy as working better (Rowan, 1976). Adverse effects on individuals which they note include feelings of inadequacy and of being excluded, and increases in destructive feelings, and in cynicism. Individuals feel that conformity is to be preferred, and that they have either to dominate others or be dominated by them. They feel unable to influence anyone and see new ideas as coming from higher in the hierarchy: they have no way of communicating with the top. However, there is a considerable difference between the way an organisation feels to those at the bottom, and the way it feels at the top. Those at the top tend to see their jobs as interesting and using their personality and skills. Those at the bottom feel bored and fatalistic, hemmed in and frustrated. Hierarchical organisations seem to prevent people getting esteem from others. There is an extreme emphasis on role separation in hierarchical organisations. Sometimes people are even called by the name of the role instead of by their own name. This could be taken to indicate that an organisation needs a particular role but does not need that particular person.

An organisation which is developing and dealing with its problems effectively is more likely to regard the open and honest expression of members' feelings as being more desirable than suppressing them. There will be increased understanding within and between working groups so suspicion decreases and there is a greater degree of trust between people in the organisation. Wasteful competition is reduced and people will work in teams more effectively. Such an organisation is characterised by wide sharing of responsibility and control. Essentially there is a process of generating valid and useful information which makes it possible for staff to make freer and more informed choices, and to feel more committed to courses of action. An organisation which seeks to move from narrow concern with cost effectiveness towards realising the potential of staff has such aims as:

1. To help set up an open, problem-solving climate throughout the organisation.
2. To seek to make sure that resources of information and competence are available for tasks where they are needed.
3. To help build trust among people throughout the organisation.
4. To increase co-operative rather than competitive efforts.
5. To foster self-determination and self-control among people in the organisation.

It has been suggested that the reason that more co-operative ways of organising social work is important is that it can lead to different ways of thinking about the field of work. From seeing clients as individuals with unique problems to be dealt with by one social worker, they can come to be seen as people with some things in common. Their problems come to be seen as ones that can be responsively tackled by any of a group of workers (Satyamurti, 1981).

Conclusion

Groupwork as a method of social work helps individuals with their social functioning. It may be distinguished from group therapy, where the emphasis is on emotional needs and psychological processes. However, it can be argued with some force that some social workers' groups are psycho-therapeutic. There is an overlap between group work and community work. It has been suggested that social work with community groups can be regarded as a form of group work when the groups are relatively small and family centred. Some groups have the aim of supporting individuals and not of facilitating personal or environmental change. Examples are groups for prisoners' wives, for parents of handicapped children, and some groups for former hospital patients. Examples of groups which aim to facilitate change include groups for offenders aimed at helping them not to offend again, groups to help people who may have been in hospital or prison to develop their social skills, and a residents' group which aims to help them live together reasonably comfortably. Other examples of 'change groups' are groups for unemployed people, for disturbed people to help them express their feelings more easily, and groups to facilitate personal growth (like encounter groups). It will be evident that many different kinds of groups come into this category, and that groups can meet a variety of needs. Working in groups has several advantages. For most people regular involvement in different kinds of groups is common, and it is also essential to meeting many material and emotional needs. Without group experience individual personality could not develop. Experience in a group can provide valuable new perceptions of individuals and their situations. Each individual is required to negotiate situations, take on roles, meet certain standards, and share feelings in a group which may be like those which he or she finds difficult in other key areas of life.

Different aspects of social processes within groups may be used by social workers, among others, to understand group dynamics. The processes involved in group formation and in its subsequent development are the formulation of group goals, the recruitment of members and the creation of the initial structure. The relations between group members have three aspects, the ranking process, sub-groupings and role structure. A third group of processes are to do with the control of the group and the exercise of authority. Further, we need to study communication and decision-making processes. There are emotional aspects of group behaviour, and the sixth important area for study is the pattern of values that evolves out of the life of any group. We need to bear in mind that conceptualising about groups in this way involves testing separately processes which interact with each other. The action is analysed by the sociologist who focuses on one or another aspect or process. These aspects of groups are also relevant in studying organisations.

Sociological studies show that the organisational aspects of social work play a more important part in influencing the provision of service than is sometimes recognised. There is evidence that how needs and problems are perceived influences social worker–client relationships. There is now a keen awareness of the structural and organisational situation in which clients and social workers are placed and of their subjective experience and response to it. Studies of clients and social workers which provide insights into these relationships have been described. Social services departments, for example, receive more requests for assistance than they can cope with adequately. While the problem for clients may be one of gaining access, for social agency staff it is often one of controlling bombardment. The various people involved have different ways of trying to cope with their respective situations. Thus it has been supposed that the structures of social services departments derive, at least in part, from the ideologies about social need held by social workers. These ideologies are general systems of ideas by means of which social workers make sense of their day-to-day practice and the administrative structure.

Considerable emphasis has been placed on more collaborative shared ways of working in social service organisations. This in part reflects the way the work group involving collaboration between members of the same or different professions is a basic feature of modern professional work. Attention has been drawn to the observation that work groups which do not function well do little to achieve the tasks for which they were established and fail to produce constructive and collaborative behaviour among their members. The cost is less than effective service to clients and lack of satisfaction among staff. It has been observed that front-line units of organisation have considerable power to make their own policy for their own work. Social workers have usually formulated objectives for their work with clients in an individual way rather than applying departmental rules. They work independently and on their own for much of their time. Their work cannot be easily overlooked by members of their organisations and it is often their decision how much of their work they discuss with senior colleagues. Operational policy is thus interpreted to a great extent through the decisions and actions of front-line workers. The form of organisational structure likely to be effective for social work is thus one where there is decision-making locally rather than centrally, evaluation of services by feedback rather than by hierarchical authority, and specialisation. However, the building of strong and cohesive neighbourhood teams may lead to problems such as hostility to outsiders and the projection of hostility on to other agencies or headquarters.

7

Social Work and the Community

Poverty and urban problems

This chapter is concerned with different dimensions of community problems. It deals with inner city problems and some lessons from community work and the problems of social isolation and loneliness. It also deals with the way sociological analysis contributes to social work intervention in social networks. Large towns and cities have poor, deprived areas which house the poorest sections of the population. These areas in themselves give rise to serious social problems. While it must be recognised that these areas do not have the monopoly of such problems they are often places where all the basic problems of society are found. Crime rates are higher in urban areas. The population is more concentrated there, and there are greater opportunities for delinquency. The rate of conviction is higher and the police are present in greater numbers. Various forms of pollution lead to problems for city dwellers. For example, environmental hazards, such as those caused by traffic, destroy amenities which are often in short supply in areas where there is greater density and congestion of population. Accommodation and housing is scarcer and therefore more expensive. Apart from ill health associated with pollution, life in cities appears to give rise to strain, anxiety and depression. Suicide rates are higher. Meyer (1976) points out that slum living in the city means more than being poor, and it has a spiralling effect on the individual:

His poverty has kept him hungry and deprived of all other basic necessities in life, but more, it has chained him to the leavings of the society at large – all of the institutional hand-me-downs finally belong to the poor. Yet slum living is more than even that: it is a living and breathing daily reminder to the individual that in an affluent society he is deprived and denigrated. In a mobile society he is trapped within his neighbourhood. In a materialistic society he is without any of its concrete rewards. In an increasingly educated society that is tooling up for the post-cybernetic age he is illiterate. In a society that strives for superior medical care he is the sickest, both mentally and physically.

The environmental ills that affect all people who live in the city affect the slum dweller more intimately, because he cannot ever find alternate modes of living or afford compensatory mechanisms to deal with them.

Most dependent people whose needs come within the remit of personal social services (the elderly, the mentally and physically ill and handicapped, families with children at risk and others) tend to be tied to their neighbourhoods because of frailty, illness, fear, handicap, low income or habit, even if there is little sense of community. A neighbourhood can be thought of as a district in which a community lives; people think of their neighbourhood as their territory. Belonging to a neighbourhood can be very important to individuals and families, even if it is a poverty-stricken inner-city slum, for example. Some very integrated neighbourhoods are found in crime-ridden places with poor or absent educational and recreational activities where unemployment is at a higher level. Studies of some slum areas have found strong social ties and friendships between residents. In these areas the territory of the home becomes extended to the streets and the external environment becomes part of the home with many personal and social activities taking place in the street. The breaking of old neighbourhood relationships is one problem of urban renewal. Others arise from the sort of housing that replaces so-called slums. The physical environment (often high-rise flats) discourages social relationships between residents as well as 'normal' family activities. People are surrounded by physical space which is not considered to be anyone's responsibility and is not supervised by any official agency. The incidence of crime against property and people is higher in these areas, and offenders are more likely not to be identified. People do not know their neighbours well enough to identify intruders, who remain anonymous.

In the 1960s the British government took a number of initiatives designed to reduce poverty. The urban aid programme was launched to give grants to voluntary and statutory organisations working to improve the education, housing, health and welfare of groups living in areas of special need. Educational Priority Areas were designated and schools in these areas were given extra staff and other resources. In 1969 the National Community Development Project (CDP) was set up. This was described as 'a neighbourhood-based experiment aimed at finding new ways of meeting the needs of people living in areas of high social deprivation'. It was assumed that problems of urban deprivation had their origins in the characteristics of local populations – in individual pathologies – and these could best be resolved by better field co-ordination of the personal social services combined with the mobilisation of self-help and mutual aid in the community. CDPs were to be established in areas of severe deprivation with local authority teams to identify needs, to promote greater co-ordination and accessibility of services at the field level, to foster community involvement and to build a communication bridge between the people and local services. Influences on CDPs were the growing emphasis on the development of professional social work and the Seebohm Report, and from the USA the first wave of anti-poverty programmes. The CDPs were located in twelve diverse areas but similar symptoms of disadvantage were found in all, indicating a familiar profile of poverty. Most areas included lower than average incomes, disproportionately high rates of unemployment, high dependence on state benefits, poor health records, poor housing, and lack of amenities. Analysis of the wider context of CDP areas confirmed that problems of multi-deprivation have to be defined in terms of structural constraints rather than psychological pathology, or external pressures rather than personal deficiencies.

It will be seen that experience gained in the British

government sponsored anti-poverty programmes contained lessons for community workers, adult educators and social workers. The idea that individual residents in declining neighbourhoods are powerless to take action to influence the processes affecting their lives was basic in the work of the CDPs. It led to two approaches in their work. One was to work at linking local areas and the agencies serving them. Initially local groups were encouraged to make their demands explicit, and this led to the involvement of people like solicitors to act as advocates and to the creation of a semi-permanent framework to serve as a neighbourhood forum. The second approach was to reinforce existing neighbourhood structures of tenants' associations, local councils, trade unions, and social clubs and to enable them to develop procedures to deal with the stresses in their neighbourhoods and to link with similar groups in their own ways.

Working with groups of local residents, providing them with information and helping them to organise and to gain access to necessary skills can be thought of not only as community work but also as adult education. This work aimed to stimulate awareness and encourage groups to press for change. In addition, the CDPs wanted to direct attention to educational practice in the school system in urban areas. By disseminating information about good practice, developing links between home and school, developing curricula relevant to local needs, the CDPs were working along similar lines to the national Education Priority Areas experiment. There has been a danger that people in the inner cities will see relief programmes as no more than the chance to obtain some additional resources to buy marginal increases in social services rather than as contributions to reconstruction. However, there have been moves away from plans geared to specific client groups to analysis of larger structural faults. If the heart of the problem is economic decline, this helps to define the limits of social services, which could be less necessary if other aspects of life are improved (Smith, 1979). In the late 1960s community workers came to place more emphasis on pressure group activity and confrontation with local and national agencies, and incorporated new theoretical perspectives about the structural nature of deprivation into their work. They saw community work as a way of giving disadvantaged people in particular a greater say in what happened to them, an aim they share with workers with an explicit socialist or Marxist orientation.

Community workers who have seen themselves as members of the social work profession emphasised self-help and liaison with local authorities. This kind of approach is illustrated by work with groups of residents on local authority housing estates in London. These groups, tenants' associations or community associations, are autonomous, plan their own programmes and manage their own finances. Such groups used consultation with community workers which helped them to make use of resources in the wider community. Consultation was offered in a way which helped groups to operate independently and to achieve their self-chosen aims. The worker's role was seen as facilitating the participation of residents in their association, engendering consensus in the committee, and this was carried out by acting as an objective observer or someone external to the group, who indicates resources needed by the group and seeks to achieve consensus between the group and outside bodies (Goetschius, 1971). This community development or professional social work approach can be related to the functionalist perspective in sociology, and these workers were employed mainly in non-statutory organisations. These 'professional' workers are mainly interested in theories of community work practice rather than macro level theories of society; they agree that community work is political but do not wish to be tied to a particular political party. Twelvetrees (1982) says that they are usually eclectic and pragmatic, using insights from a range of disciplines such as psychology, political science and organisational and urban sociology to inform the use of relationship, planning, organisational and action skills. He points out that some social workers have reservations about the unitary approach. Many community workers object to it either because they see it as a way by which social work tries to colonise community work, or because they regard it as too readily glossing over the differences in the objectives of, and the skills needed for, different forms of intervention. Community workers of the 'socialist' school regard community work as part of a class struggle, their principal aims being to raise class consciousness and help working-class organisations gain more power over institutions which affect their lives, a perspective which emerged particularly from the experience of the Community Development Projects.

Loneliness and social work

The idea that modern urban living makes for loneliness has to be regarded with caution. It is difficult to assess whether a single mother living in a high-rise block of flats with small children is any more lonely and depressed than her Victorian counterpart. But we often read that loneliness is really the most serious problem facing society, with ten million people finding it hard to relate to others, being fearful of going out, and many finding it hard to admit to being lonely in case it means there is something wrong with them. It is helpful to distinguish between situational loneliness, which may be aggravated by living in a high-rise flat or being a single parent, and chronic loneliness, caused by individual psychological problems. It may be a mistake simply to blame the problem on the stress of modern living. It is probably impossible to estimate the extent of loneliness in our society today, since it is a self-perceived problem. Loneliness is not synonymous with solitude but involves a conscious lack of friendship, warmth and human contact, often accompanied by a feeling of being different or unworthy, exacerbated by difficulties in forming satisfactory relationships with other people. It seems that about twenty-five per cent of the population is lonely, with women, the elderly, the young, the single parents, the widowed and the unemployed being most at risk.

MORI (Market and Opinion Research International) carried out a poll (interviewing) a quota sample of 1801 people over fifteen throughout the UK in November 1982; its main finding is that a quarter of Britain's 44 million adults are sometimes lonely. Asked whether they felt at all lonely, 76 per cent said 'No', and 24 per cent said 'Yes'. They ranged from the 4 per cent who felt lonely every day, to the 3 per cent who felt lonely less than once a year. Fourteen per cent, or 6 million people, said that they felt lonely at least once a month. Lonely people have fewer family members with whom they can talk. When there is a bereavement in the family they will turn to relatives for help and advice, but will be more likely than most people to look for some support from social services or from their doctors. One in five lonely people sees a doctor at least once a month, whereas in the population as a whole one person in nine goes as often. Twice as many women as men (32 per cent as against 16 per cent) are sometimes lonely. This is still a minority of the population, but it is a problem which affects one in every three women and one in six men. Loneliness appears to be more common in the 15–24 age group, becomes less common in middle age, and then becomes more common again among people over 65. The most common cause of loneliness, mentioned by 59 per cent of those surveyed, was the death of a close friend or relative. The poll thus seems to suggest that it is the absence of loved people who have died rather than the absence of the living which causes so much loneliness in our society at present.

Chronic loneliness is an internal psychological problem. Yet social isolation can be the fault of an uncaring society. Elderly people can often be lonely, but this is apparently because there are so many of them. In 1951 there were 1.7 million people over 75 in Great Briatin compared with 3.2 million in 1983. Families still provide most care for the elderly and disabled. Only 5 per cent are in institutions – about the same proportion as in pre-Welfare State days. In many areas social services provide a range of services for elderly people living alone, and there are also voluntary organisations providing sheltered housing and other help and in many areas visiting schemes are organised. Although social mobility has probably contributed to the breakup of the extended family and friendship networks, this was also true at some time in the past. During the last twenty years self-help groups have mushroomed and they are one answer to situational loneliness. Whatever the problems isolating an individual from wider society, self-help groups act both as pressure groups to obtain better treatment and facilities and to provide social contacts for people in a similar situation.

Polansky (1980) and Hopkins (1982) have suggested that the major focus of social work should be understanding and treatment of loneliness, and that the skill of social workers lies in that area. They have argued that the consistent feature of social work practice, whether social workers are employed to work directly with clients or whether they participate in other activities undertaken by the agency, is the easing of loneliness, and social work also aims to facilitate the use of other services that are available. Social workers are required to perform a range of different tasks. They are expected to assess eligibility for aids for handicapped people, assess the cause and extent of physical injuries to children, to collect fine payments, establish welfare rights, arrange convalescence and negotiate the reconnection of gas and electricity. Such activities are also carried out by people other than social workers, many of whom are better qualified to do them – for example, welfare rights workers, occupational therapists and paediatricians. It is not the end of social work to provide the multitude of social services, but it can be thought of as the means to the end of helping to ease loneliness. For many people the social worker helps them get back in touch with others: the social worker may be the person of last resort who understands how they have felt shunned by others.

People other than social workers can be more effective in achieving the instrumental aims of small groups (as in intermediate treatment, for example). People other than social workers are better suited to achieve the instrumental aims of community-based groups (as in residents' committees or playgroups), and others also help to care for residents in homes or hostels or people in day centres. Social workers have as their prime focus the effect of group experience on the people involved, either in helping people to gain insight into the ways they handle their relationships or as a way of easing loneliness experienced elsewhere. Social workers focus on the separation of individuals or groups from others in the community and work directly to ease this loneliness. They try to ease loneliness by creating opportunities for new attachments and easing the strain on present ones. The latter is not the prime function of household management or nursing. Practice in residential care is informed by understanding the ways in which daily living experiences serve to bring people closer together or distance them further. Admission to care is likely to heighten a person's awareness of separation from those with whom he felt he belonged, and from familiar places and their associations. This suggests that the careworker will take into account how the newcomer handled past experiences of separation and the fear of loss and will bear in mind that the client has preconceptions about residential care. It also suggests, to take another example, that discharging clients without first ensuring their place in the lives of others negates the experience of interdependence at the heart of residential social work practice. In moving beyond the establishment, residents should not be moved out of reach or out of the mind of those with whom they belong. There are implications for staff. They need not only to attend to the loneliness of residents, but also to be able to share their own experiences with each other, if they are to avoid isolation themselves (Hopkins, 1984).

Understanding social networks

The idea of community social work and working with formal and informal systems of care makes sense. But it faces the social worker in practice with how sociological analysis provides an effective response to clients' needs. How are clients' support networks to be identified? The social worker needs instruments to analyse the adequacy or inadequacy of clients' social networks. One of the largest resources in the community is often the help available from friends, relatives and neighbours. Supportive relationships only exist through the links between individuals (their social networks). But the systems of relatives, neighbours or voluntary groups do not in themselves provide support: it depends on the meaning the links have for the members of these systems. It cannot be assumed that because someone has many other people around him he must be receiving more support than someone with few people around him. The support that an individual perceives himself as receiving is as significant as the actual

amount of support he receives. Relationships are not necessarily universal in meeting all needs. A close relationship with
a partner, for example, does not compensate for the absence
of wider social contacts. And there is not a clear distinction
between relationships which are frequent, close and warm
and those which are concerned with economic, health or work
needs and of little emotional importance. A social network
involves costs as well as benefits for an individual. Thus, while
family relationships provide members with satisfactions not
available to socially isolated people, they also produce a set of
obligations and constraints which may have a cost to an
individual's mental health. Thus increased integration into
the family can lead to relapse rather than improvement for
some schizophrenic patients.

McCallister and Fischer (1978) (quoted by Taylor and
Huxley, 1984) defined the immediate network as the set of
people who are most likely to be sources of a variety of
rewarding interactions such as discussing a personal problem,
borrowing money or social recreation. They devised questions to discover the names of people who fulfil these needs in
a way which added different network members, that is, names
not already elicited by other questions. The questions
covered the following topics.

1. Who would care for the respondent's home if they
   went out of town.
2. If they work, with whom they talk about work decisions.
3. Who, if anyone, had helped with household tasks in
   the last three months.
4. With whom they engaged in social activities (like
   inviting home for dinner, or going to a movie).
5. Whom they talk with about hobbies.
6. If unmarried, who their fiancé(e) or 'best friend' is.
7. With whom they talk about personal worries.
8. Whose advice they consider in making important
   decisions.
9. From whom they could or would borrow a large sum of
   money.

10. Enumeration of adult members of the respondents' households.

The social worker has to analyse the structure of the clients' social groupings. Does the single parent feel isolated because she knows only a few people, because she does not see them very often, because she has no close intimate persons in her network, or because such people live at a distance and are thus inaccessible? Is she isolated because her network consists of a small group and does not provide links to other networks so that she can meet new people? Does her isolation result from problems in communicating with other members of the network – for example, because of lack of mobility or of a telephone? Are enough people available to provide her with support but does she subjectively see this as inadequate? These are the kinds of questions to consider in understanding the kinds of support needed by clients. A study which dealt with the role of social stress in puerperal depression rated social support available to out-patients (Paykel *et al.*, 1980). They were asked:

(a) how much they could tell their husbands about their worries and problems and how much husbands would listen or avoid this (adequacy of communication with husband);
(b) how much help their husbands gave with household tasks and the care of children (help from husband); and
(c) whether they had someone in whom they could confide who was receptive and easily available (adequacy of confidante).

The use of the concept of social network, discussed in various parts of this book, is examined in relation to individuals, relatives and neighbours by Ballard and Rosser (1979). They show how the practice method of network assembly involves bringing together in one place as many neighbours and relatives of a person in need of help as possible. The idea is to discover and develop networks to encourage people to solve their own problems, and also to create practical resources to overcome such problems as social and physical isolation, work and recreational difficulties and loneliness. It is important to note that bringing together a number of people like this can involve difficulties. These include family rivalries, disputes between neighbours, marital and other difficulties and, in addition, people may feel guilty about not having done more to help others in the network. Experience in general suggests that an assembly should be used when a client is at a point of crisis. Members of the network must also feel that the situation is serious enough to justify a meeting of this kind. Ballard and Rosser (1979) emphasise the importance of the positive commitment of social workers to using this idea. Rapid social change has fragmenting effects on the social networks of individuals. The destructive effects of urban planning and slum clearance, rapid social mobility, high-rise flats and the development of new housing estates can precipitate distress and create tensions for individuals and families. Social workers often feel apathetic or apprehensive about trying to make an impact on such problems, partly because of their experience of their own networks being disrupted by successive reorganisations. Their networks may themselves be atrophied, and the bureaucracy in which they try to work may have stunted their willingness to pursue new initiatives. Social network analyses used in sociological research are often lengthy, but they can be adapted for use in social work practice. This is illustrated in a paper by Taylor and Huxley (1984). They suggest that the questions below can provide useful information in making assessments. They also provide a focus for discussion with clients about what kinds of deficiencies are felt in their social relationships. By naming people it is possible to ascertain the degree of connectedness within the network and to identify clusters within it, and thus to trace patterns of relationships. If used at different points in time it also enables the social worker and client to make some measure of change or to evaluate the effectiveness of interventions such as joining a group. The questions suggested are as follows:

Name	Frequency of contact	Status, e.g. relative, friend, neighbour
1. How many people do you know who could come to see you at any time and would not mind if the house was untidy or you were in the middle of a meal?		
2. Are there people you can lean on in times of difficulty and know that they can be relied upon to give you real help? (Personal help not just practical assistance.)		
3. Is there any one person without whom life would be intolerable?		
4. When you are worried or in a difficult situation is there anyone you go to for advice or guidance?		
5. Is there anyone who tells you or makes you feel that you are good at things you do at home or at work or with others?		
6. Which of all the people you have mentioned know each other? (Know – have contact with each other independently of you.)		

Conclusion

It has been recognised that social workers operate in conditions of material distress. Poverty is still widespread and it is often related to particular age groups such as elderly people and families with dependent children; single parent families particularly are affected. There is a tendency for social workers' clients to come from sections of the population affected by declining urban areas and by a wide spectrum of social problems such as poor education provision and facilities for children and young people, unemployment, a low level of health and social services provision and large-scale homelessness. It is apparent that social workers may be able to do little directly about a social context of deprivation and they may feel overwhelmed by the difficulties they face. Sociological analysis should enable them to take a broader view and it should help in discerning primarily economic factors in situations and not lead to a closed political view. In this chapter, and in the book as a whole, I have emphasised the ways in which social and personal problems are inter-linked. They are perceived as having different effects at different social levels. Dealing with problems of poverty means addressing broad social issues about incomes and the Welfare State, taxation and the class system. Emphasis is placed on changing social structures at the macro-social level as the basis for reducing inequality and poverty. But this has to be complemented by changes in individuals and neighbour-hood groups, as they try to adapt to changing social influences and to resist or initiate changes themselves.

In the previous chapter as well as in this one I referred to misgivings which have been expressed (for example, by Glastonbury, 1975) about the appropriateness of hierarchical structures for social service organisations. The basic argu-ment is that for their effective operation social services require a concentration of authority and resources at the front line. It calls into question the usefulness of present hierar-chical structures. The disadvantages of bureaucratic organ-isations, including the consolidation of decision-making in members of the hierarchy, the possibility that the self-interest of members takes precedence over service objectives and the pressures towards conformity are very real. These problems have been seen in the way social service departments have been organised and in pressure to change them. This pressure has been increased as emphasis has come to be placed on local community participation. This involvement in social service organisations and use of resources makes it very desirable that decision-making power and control of resources should be decentralised. To achieve more open and responsive welfare agencies, reducing or changing the domination of hierarchies is necessary. A more open structure requires all staff and people from outside the agency to take part. An essential feature of polyarchic arrangements is that they assume collective ways of working and it means that a group has to work out how it will divide up tasks among members. This in turn requires an open acknowledgement by the group of the strengths and weaknesses of individual members.

Urban renewal has its problems in the form of dislocation of territory and the destruction of social networks. Social workers involved with families in this situation are aware of these problems. Although a family's situation seems to be unpleasant or intolerable to social workers it may be wholly acceptable to the family. Social workers involved with families who are being moved and rehoused need to take this into account and to investigate whether there are differences in their values and expectations. While caution is advisable in making sweeping generalisations about loneliness it has been suggested that modern urban living contributes to the problem. It has been suggested that the skill of social workers and their major focus lies in understanding and helping to ease loneliness. Sociological analysis is of help in understanding human systems which involve various patterns of interaction between people. Social workers try to reconnect people or bring them into systems and try to ease the sense of separation that may exist between the client and others. They recognise that relieving one tension may create stress elsewhere. Social workers thus need to be well informed about the neighbourhoods in which they work and can use this knowledge in the development of relationships in the community and in other ways. I have examined ways in which social workers may assess the adequacy or inadequacy of social networks.

The increased emphasis on the community outlined in this book has meant that social workers try to involve members of the community in caring. In part this means continuing and enhancing organised voluntary activities such as those integrating handicapped people, the work of bodies like Age Concern, and the development of self-help groups for ex-hospital patients. It has been suggested that increased community participation in residential establishments might draw more attention to their inadequacies and the distressing situations in which residents may exist. Collective self-help and the mobilisation of neighbourhood resources is needed if help is to be offered to people in need, and this greater community involvement in caring could lead to greater local control over available services. The broader, community-orientated view of social work I have taken in this book implies several things. It suggests, for example, that social workers try to reduce the fragmentation found in many social services agencies. It suggests that social workers work with neighbourhood groups as well as individuals and families. This approach to working with social networks requires staff to adopt a team approach. I suggest that sociology makes an important and relevant contribution to dealing with these subjects and thus to the development of social work practice.

8

Social Work Practice and Sociology

Problems in reconstructing social work

In concluding a book which has covered a variety of approaches in sociology I should like to underline the dynamic nature of the subject. Recently, natural and social scientists have questioned many mainstream ideas and assumptions about their disciplines, including taken-for-granted notions about the character of knowledge. Brittan (1973) writes that 'an adequate and relevant sociology respects the social world – the empirical reality with which it is engaged.' This empirical reality does not consist of the beautifully elegant constructions of contemporary research methodology but of the actual living life of men in the course of their everyday interaction. This everyday life cannot be reduced to the level of pointer readings on measuring instruments, nor can it be described in terms of pushes, urges, stimuli, responses and the inevitability of historical forces. It can only be understood in its own terms. And this under-standing involves the ability to recognise the human world for what it is!' primarily as the world in which men act towards each other in meaningful terms.'

The controversial subjects addressed here do not lend themselves to a brisk summing-up, and it is to be expected that argument will continue. It is not surprising to find that the newer approaches in sociology which I have characterised as interactionist and critical are not easily accepted. Their potential influence on the organisation and practice of social work is potentially great, but it is not easy to follow through their radical implications. In the first place they emphasise that theorists should be self-critical, thus recognising that the ways in which social work practices are conceptualised depend on more than the theoretical orientations of social workers. The variety of accounts of the nature of social work, of what theories are valid and relevant and the absence of a unitary philosophical basis for practice may be attributed to these factors. Secondly, they suggest that theory and practice influence each other. Practice provides a way of evaluating theoretical orientations because it has built-in values. Some orientations could be ruled out if they led directly to or sanctioned behaviour that exploited or ignored people. Thus they question the propensity to see theory and practice as unified and monolithic entities. This rigid separation seems to have more to do with the unproductive way we organise academics and practitioners than with recognition of the problems in the relationship between theorising and practising. Contemporary views of social work practice as based on 'knowledge' drawn largely from the social sciences and on moral principles are unsatisfactory. The use of medical and unitary models, for example, as ways of thinking about social work practice maintain inflexible boundaries between social science knowledge and understanding of underlying values. They maintain the artificial separation of theory, values and action of which social work is constituted. They tend to ignore other theories and ideologies and the way they sometimes conflict with one another. The search for unitary theories and for technical expertise may helpfully be seen in relation to aspirations to exclusive professional status. These involve consistent attempts to extend or develop the 'knowledge' base or, at least, to appear to do this. The interests of the people who try to use social services and the people who staff them cannot be identical, but the attempts to creat partnerships between them by the British Association of Social Workers are remarkable developments.

It is understandable that for rather a long time social workers have shared fairly simple ideas about the prevention and treatment of social problems. Ingenious researchers, though they may not have shared illusory expectations that such problems could be dealt with easily, have implied that once causal factors were identifid they could be dealt with in some way. They seem to have assumed that the social sciences were closely similar to the natural sciences, and that through the steady accumulation of 'knowledge' of 'social reality' psycho-social problems could be eliminated. Many, if not all, such problems seemed to be transformed into technical questions about the relationships between variables which lend themselves to technical control. The newer orientations challenge such views on the ground that they misrepresent human behaviour and social issues. They suggest that social issues cannot be properly described nor understood unless the meanings that behaviour and psycho-social problems have for the people involved, and the ways in which they interpret their own actions and the actions of others, are taken into account. An adequate understanding of social life involves trying to discover and uncover the ways in which people understand themselves and interpret what they are doing. This involves asking if there are distortions or ideological mystifications in people's understandings.

Notions of 'knowledge' of 'social reality' as monolithic entities were challenged by Berger and Kellner (1982) who argued that social reality is not 'out there' waiting to be experienced by social actors, even though it may often feel as though it is. Rather, people actively construct or create different social realities through social interaction and they then seem to exist independently and to influence behaviour from outside. Social realities are regarded as inter-subjective – they exist in the consciousness of people who can share meanings and interpretations. Thus people are seen as active and purposeful and not simply subject to outside forces over which they have no control at all. Although the interpretations and choices which people make are affected by structural factors outside the control of individuals, the reasons for their actions are thus found in how they perceive events. They are not always found in some pattern of objective laws that act as external determinants of behaviour. The view that social work can gain from the different newer social science perspectives has been defended by Sheppard (1984) who proposes criteria for their application. They may be applied: (i) by focusing on problems confronted by social workers – for example, child abuse; and (ii) in the light of problems of social work – for example, its nature, justification and effectiveness.

The challenge of interactionist and critical perspectives

Another important development has been the realisation that an adequate understanding of society must be critical. This has been expressed by Bernstein (1976):

> We are coming to realise that human rationality cannot be limited to technical and instrumental reason: that human beings can engage in rational argumentation in which there is a commitment to the critical evaluation of the quality of human life: that we can cultivate theoretical discourse in which there is a rational discussion of the conflict of critical interpretations, and practical discourse in which human beings try not simply to manipulate and control one another but to understand one another genuinely and work together toward practical – not technical – ends.

Critical theorists question the idea of cumulative progress in the social sciences and positivist approaches in particular. They see all forms of scientific enquiry as being socially located and as contributing to the maintenance of social order. They do not see science as disinterested and neutral. Rather, they perceive mainstream social science in the context of exploitative and oppressive social structures, and argue that it could and should assume a liberating role in reforming oppressive institutions and in achieving radical change in society. This position is based on the idea that values inevitably affect the work of social scientists, and it is important to be clear what those values are. Since all knowledge of social life is partial and favours somebody, social scientists should be explicit about favouring people whose voices are seldom or never heard because they are powerless. Some critical theorists go further and argue that it is not enough just to help people have their say. People who are exploited need to learn how to throw off their oppressors, and social scientists should help them to achieve this. The movement towards more direct engagement in political action may not be particularly novel but is certainly seen in recent developments in social work. Clarke (1979) noted that attempts by the state to cut welfare, to increase welfare workers' 'productivity' and to increase the repressive elements of their work have produced collective responses and resistances which could potentially move beyond narrow conceptions of practice. Critical theories focus on the processes of social work practice and the contradictions that are inherent in it. They note the contemporary narrow interpretation of social work as getting the job done, and that social workers are often unable to look at the wider context in which their work takes place. They see the work organisation as ensuring that social workers are sufficiently preoccupied by immediate tasks that they do not consider the broader picture. They see social workers as being de-skilled into functionaries operating bureaucratic routines. This situation has been characterised by Gammack (1985) as a tragic pantomime, and his comments may be applied to social work education as well as to practice. He argues that caring is not just an end product of 'people and paper pushing', but the expression of a comprehensive personal system in which people are able to care because they are upheld by a total ethos in which caring is the norm. This appears to be a remote possibility because social work can only be practised in circumstances of organisational integrity. Gammack sees the heavy boots of legalism, control and routinisation as undermining the provision of help and care for those in need.

Some of the humanistic implications of interactionist and critical theories for social work practice may be seen in questioning of the validity and relevance of unitary approaches. Hardiker and Barker (1981) find it very difficult to excavate the ways in which they can and should be incorporated into social work's purposes and activities. The problems in general were earlier summarised by Wolin (1968):

Systems theories, communication theories, structural-functional theories are unpolitical theories shaped by the desire to explain certain forms of non-political phenomena. They offer no significant choice or critical analysis of the

quality, direction or fate of public life. Where they are not
alien intrusions, they share the same uncritical – and
therefore untheoretical – assumptions of the prevailing
ideology as that which justified the present 'authoritative
allocation of values' in our society.

It has to be accepted that particular theoretical approaches
are not necessarily associated with particular value systems.
Individuals formulate theories and ideologies and choose to
subscribe to certain values. The point was made earlier that
relationships between values and theoretical orientations are
complicated, but we have to admit that the growing interest in
unitary theories among social workers has paralleled growth
in the size and complexity of social services departments.
Hierarchical patterns of supervision and control and increasing centralised direction have caused concern to probation
officers too. It has to be recognised that moves towards
increasing bureaucratisation cannot be explained in simple
terms since many different interests are involved. One
current controversial issue, however, is clearly the appropria-
tion of selected social and personal problems by politicians of
any persuasion. This opens up an entirely new area of debate
which cannot be dealt with in this book. What seems to be
relevant in the present context is that this may be an
important influence on social services staff at all levels. They
seem to have placed more and more emphasis on rules,
regulations and procedures, and the widespread preoccupa-
tion with management has been reflected in the growing use
of legal terms and words like tasks, goals and targets to
describe relationships between people. The values that have
come to be associated with much local authority social work
are orderliness, rationalisation, predictability and bureaucratic control. Staff in social services appear to be constrained
by day-to-day monitoring of their activities and with concentration on routine responses to requests for assistance. High
priority is given to the maintenance of the organisation and
the defence of staff from questioning and criticism. This may
be related to the lack of full awareness, sometimes on the part
of people who try to use social services, of the options
available to them. They may feel that they have to agree to

terms which can restrict social workers to dealing with certain 'problems' defined administratively and over limited spans of time, or they may be manoeuvred into accepting such terms. Obviously social workers are subject to powerful pressures within their organisations to accept certain norms, and these may conflict with professional and/or personal beliefs.

Alongside these developments the idea of unitary theories of social work practice has been popular. The concept of system has been seen as central to understanding social structures and relationships at macro as well as micro levels. These theories stress stability and the maintenance of order, and society is seen as a collection of individuals in units of various sizes all interacting in mutual harmony. Unitary theories, then, are based on a conservative ideology which assumes that social equlibrium is basically healthy and that most conflicts between people at different social levels can be worked out without making basic changes in structures or institutions. Unitary theories are thus based on assumptions of social consensus and agreed moral values and uphold existing power relationships and the *status quo*. These theories are defective in their inability to analyse conflict in family and community structures and exploitative relationships. This may be illustrated by the value judgement that the family is 'best' which underlies policies of community care which often depend on care by relatives. Usually there is one carer, who is often female, although unmarried sons may care for elderly parents, and husbands for disabled wives. The burdens placed on some families lead to conflict and stress to the extent of breakdowns in health or the break-up of the family unit, a partner or children leaving home because they cannot tolerate the situation any longer.

I think that the unitary theorists' assumptions that it is desirable to encourage adaptation within the existing system is open to question. The problem is that maintaining the *status quo* may be profoundly disadvantageous to the interests of the client and/or members of the family. This line of thinking is supported by feminists, for whom adjustments in the outlook or circumstances of women within the system to maintain the *status quo* leads to them becoming more deeply involved in an oppressive social structure. Feminists perceive assumptions about women's inferior position in the family and at work as being accepted by unitary theorists and reinforced in current social work practice. It is clear that unitary approaches are not helpful to those who want to challenge traditional ideas. These theories tend to reinforce strategies used by social workers to deal with tensions around their control functions such as sustaining stereotypes of clients, maintaining distance from them and by using apparently neutral approaches such as administrative requirements. This point of view is reflected in the work of some writers on social work. For example, Ragg (1977) and Wilkes (1981) do not see the individual as an object to be scientifically analysed, manipulated and controlled, but as conscious, rational and as transcending objective analysis. They see people as having qualities which are beyond what can be predicted or controlled. People can choose how to act, whether they behave responsibly or not, and they can thus contribute to determining their own nature through their response to moral claims and cultural influences. They can choose whether or not to act altruistically and disinterestedly.

New orientations and their effects on practice

There is much in current practice to justify concern about a lack of authenticity in worker–client relationships. There is a real risk that the social worker's concern for her client as a fellow human being is impossible to express or will be extinguished by practising an occupational role in state bureaucracies and emphasising technical efficiency at the expense of personal relationships. Interactionist and critical theories could contribute to radical thinking about the organisation and practice of social work. I have noted that obstacles to this may be found in contemporary economic, political and social values which affect practice and the ways social workers perceive and think about clients' social situations. This is crucial because a blinkered professionalism is probably as dangerous as exclusive concern with macro-social change. Both may ignore or undervalue the individual. Although the use of these different theoretical frameworks is not necessarily mutually exclusive, it may be difficult to use more than one at a time (Whittington and Holland, 1985). Their use, then, does not result in a unified social work perspective but they offer ways of analysing constructions of social reality which find their expressions in policy and practice.

In challenging social workers to question and dismantle bureaucratic and administrative rigidities and technical orthodoxy, they provide potential for changing stereotyped and habitual responses. I have discussed interactionists' concern with social realities and with the meanings through which social interaction takes place. They have stressed the part language plays in the ways people construct a meaningful world out of their experience. From this theoretical point of view social relationships are examined as the meeting of various views of reality with a view to discovering why some realities prevail over others. The interactionist can study the vocabularies and ideologies of various groups whether the problem is to understand how offenders are labelled and treated or how social workers categorise needs. Social workers have adopted medical terminology in describing the problems or needs of their clients. Problems, for example, may be referred to as symptoms, and terms such as 'treatment strategy' are used to refer to helping actions intended to remove symptoms or to meet the clients' needs. The medical model serves to isolate the problem a person presents. The idea of the individual needs of sick people has tended to become generalised and to shape definitions of needs in a number of professions, including social work.

Usually changes in descriptive labels or terms represent shifts in ideological positions. Although clients do not have symptoms as patients do, they are perceived as deficient in some ways and as needing to develop social skills, assertiveness, or to realise their potential in some way. The new language perpetuates some of the assumptions of the medical model, in particular ideas about the nature of the power relationships between social worker and client. If you study the ways in which disabled or handicapped people have been referred to and classified over the years you find that the vocabulary contains mechanical and non-human terms. In the early twentieth century idiots and feeble-minded people were mentioned as 'damaged goods'. In contemporary publications these connotations are often perpetuated, so that someone with Down's syndrome is referred to in 1985 as 'needing repair'. This kind of language effectively maintains distance from other people so as to preserve the comfort of those not evidently disabled, and encourages us to think about people in mechanistic ways.

If a radical change in orientation was achieved it would involve looking at individual needs in the social context in different ways, and going further than looking at an individual's social skills and sources of social support in terms of administrative categories. The interactionist approach stresses the integrity of the self and the individual's sense of her own identity. This orientation, then, is developmental and dynamic and regards behaviour as an outcome of various personal and inter-personal forces, and it seeks to take account of the whole person in her social context.

Moving away from mainstream models involves changes in the ways assessments are made. Categorisations of needs in terms of organisational requirements would be challenged and they would be expressed in ways which would combine clients' subjective experiences and observations of others. Needs and problems are not necessarily expressed in individual terms, although this is obviously appropriate sometimes, but may be in terms of the experience of the group or family in relation to the individual's behaviour or it may be in terms of the communication patterns which an individual has learned to use in the group or family context. Intervention is then carried out so as to help with the problems perceived by the individual, but it also aims to influence the group in such a way that inter-personal conflict is modified. These techniques are currently used by many family therapists and group workers whose theoretical orientations may also include behavioural modification or psycho-analysis, communication or role theory. Behaviour is thus seen as a consequence of an individual's interactions with others, and communications between people are a main focus of the social worker's attention. These ways of helping thus involve a different orientation to people, who are seen as influenced by social processes: a range of techniques is used.

The influences on the social worker and the roles of professional helpers are questioned, not only by members of ethnic or other minority groups and poor people, but also by supervisors and social workers themselves. The tidy appearance given to processes of helping by some theoretical approaches is questioned by the newer perspectives referred to in this book. The sequence of acquiring 'the facts' about a situation, analysing them, selecting a plan of intervention and formulating goals is not necessarily the process which occurs in practice. Social workers who can be responsive to feedback as they make services available are constantly able to increase their understanding of varied social norms and structures. They can then develop new ways of understanding the nature of distress experienced by individuals and groups. They may also be led to greater awareness of ways in which procedures may need to be changed, and for work to be re-defined so as to make more flexible responses which are not constrained by technical and theoretical rigidity.

Conclusion

It seems peculiarly appropriate in the context in which this book has been written to refer to the advice of the much-quoted American sociologist C. Wright Mills (1978):

> Above all, do not give up your moral and political autonomy by accepting in somebody else's terms the illiberal practicality of the bureaucratic ethos or the liberal practicality of the moral scatter. Know that many personal troubles cannot be solved merely as troubles but must be understood in terms of the public issues – and in terms of the problems of history making. Know that the human meaning of public issues must be revealed by relating them to personal troubles – and to the problems of the individual life. Know that the problems of social science, when adequately formulated, must include both troubles and issues. . . .

Further Reading

Chapter 1

There is no shortage of books about different sociological perspectives and methods. Worsley (1976) is an established textbook which is widely used and which has been revised since it was first published. Fletcher (1974) provides a lively account of three sociological approaches. Berger and Berger (1978) and Bilton (1981) are both also useful for the subject of this chapter.

Chapter 2

There is a voluminous literature on social policy, of course. Reading of relevance to social workers' everyday concerns includes the paper by Finch and Groves (1980). It is also helpful to read George and Wilding (1976) and Wilding's (1981) book on professional power. On specific issues the books edited by Cheetham (1982) and Worsley (1981) are both useful to social workers.

The book edited by Walker (1984) and that by Jones, Brown and Bradshaw (1983) are both helpful on the subject matter of this chapter, and so is the article by Land (1978). There is a tendency in much research into illness and disability to separate out matters relating to health and to study them in isolation from other aspects of social life. A study of twenty-four individuals which tries to give a theoretical as well as a descriptive account of their ideas and theories about illness and health services is by Cornwall (1984). The author explores the relationship between these ideas and the social factors influencing the peoples' lives. The book focuses on deteriorating standards of care in the inner city and on subjects' social networks, and is thus relevant to several topics referred to in this text.

Chapter 3

Two basic texts on group theory which can be recommended are by Bion (1961) and Cartwright and Zander (1968). Warham (1977) is of help in representing large complex organisations as institutions having political and sociological dimensions, and she discusses concepts of bureaucracy and professionalism.

Chapter 4

To develop this chapter Siporin (1975) may be helpful. Interactionist approaches are discussed by Fitzjohn (1974) and Smith (1975). The book edited by Cheetham (1982) deals with ethnicity and social work in a positive way. Minuchin (1974) is still an important source on family social work. Borkowski, Murch and Walker (1983) is useful on marital violence. The literature on family and community violence and disorganisation increases steadily, and in fast developing fields such as this students need to keep abreast with the relevant journals and be alert to book reviews. A practical guide on problems of child abuse and sexual abuse is edited for the CIBA Foundation by Porter (1984). It analyses family characteristics and gives examples of various approaches to intervention. There are chapters on professional attitudes and co-operation and links between professional and family networks. Publications by the professional bodies (for example, the guide on non-accidental injury by the British Association of Social Workers in 1985) are often useful.

Chapter 5

Payne (1979), Parry, Rustin and Satyamurti (1979) and Walker and Beaumont (1981) are useful on social control aspects of social work. Howe (1980) and Sainsbury (1982) are relevant to discussion of social work as an occupation. Wilding (1981) and Wilkes (1981) are thought-provoking on contemporary issues, while Heraud (1979) is regarded as a basic resource.

Chapter 6

The book by Davies (1975) provides a useful overview of groupwork and is a valuable source book. It can usefully be read in conjunction with Douglas (1978), Brown (1979), Heap (1985) and Whitaker (1985). On working in organisations, Adamson (1983) and Brazer and Holloway (1978) are recommended.

Chapter 7

Of several authoritative books, those by Holman (1978), Townsend (1979), Field (1981) and Donnison (1982) are recommended. Meyer (1976) discusses the place of social work in a clear way, and Hopkins (1982 and 1984) repays reading on loneliness. Among publications seeking to understand the meaning of community social work in practice, the booklet by Henderson, Scott and their co-workers (1984) identifies growth points and obstacles to development. They argue that as well as conceptual changes, community social work required major organisational changes, and they outline policy and training implications. The book edited by Whittaker and Garbarino (1983) examines mainly American experience of the workings of networks. It shows how the orientations of professionals towards dyadic intervention, for example, have been changing, and how they have been involving people in their own care over quite a long period. Baldock (1983) and Hadley and McGrath (1981) on patch teams, and Taylor and Huxley (1984) on the analysis of social networks, should be useful.

Chapter 8

Bernstein (1976), Brooke and Davis (1985), Statham (1978) and Walker and Beaumont (1981) are helpful.

References and Bibliography

Abel Smith, B. (1960) *A History of the Nursing Profession*, London, Heinemann.

Abrams, P. and McCulloch, A. (1980) 'Men, women and communes', in M. Anderson (ed.), *Sociology of the Family*, Harmondsworth, Penguin.

Ackhurst, C. et. al. (1980) 'Dear Priscilla Young . . .', *Community Care*, no. 318.

Adamson, F. (1983) 'Inside the work group', in J. Lishman (ed.), *Collaboration and Conflict: Working with Others*, Research Highlights, no. 7, University of Aberdeen.

Albrow, M. (1970) *Bureaucracy* London, Macmillan.

Algie, J. (1970) 'Management and organisation in the social services', *British Hospital Journal and Social Service Review*, 26 June.

Algie, J. (1975) *Social Values, Objectives and Action*, London, Kogan Page.

Alinsky, S. (1972) *Rules for Radicals*, New York, Vintage Books.

Anderson, D. (1982) *Social Work and Mental Handicap*, London, Macmillan.

Argyle, M. (1978) *The Psychology of Interpersonal Behaviour*, Harmondsworth, Penguin.

Argyris, C. (1970) *Intervention Theory and Method*, Reading, Mass., Addison-Wesley.

Baher, E. et. al. (1974) *At Risk: An Account of the Work of the Battered Child Research Team*, London, NSPCC.

Baldock, P. (1983) 'Patch systems: a radical change for the better?', in I. Sinclair and D. N. Thomas (eds), *Perspectives on Patch*, London, National Institute for Social Work.

Ballard, R. and Rosser, P. (1979) 'Social network assembly', in D. Brandon and B. Jordan (eds), *Creative Social Work*, Oxford, Blackwell.

Bamford, T. (1982) *Managing Social Work*, London, Tavistock.

Barclay Report (1982) *Social Workers: Their Roles and Tasks*, London, Bedford Square Press.

Barmby, P. (1982) 'Academic worlds apart', *Social Work Today*, vol. 13, no. 43.

Barton, R. (1976) *Institutional Neurosis*, Bristol, John Wright.

142 *References and Bibliography*

Benton, R., Clifford, P., Frash, S., Lousada, J. and Rosenthall, J. (1985) *The Politics of Mental Health*, London, Macmillan.
Berger, P. (1966) *Invitation to Sociology*, Harmondsworth, Penguin.
Berger, P. and Berger, B. (1978) *Sociology: A Biographical Approach*, Harmondsworth, Penguin.
Berger, P. L. and Kellner, H. (1970) 'Marriage and the construction of reality', in H. P. Dreitzel (ed.), *Recent Sociology*, London, Macmillan.
Berger, P. L. and Kellner, H. (1982) *Sociology Reinterpreted*, Harmondsworth, Penguin.
Bernstein, R. J. (1976) *The Restructuring of Social and Political Theory*, Oxford, Blackwell.
Bilton, T. et. al. (1981) *Introductory Sociology*, London, Macmillan.
Bion, W. R. (1961) *Experiences in Groups*, London, Tavistock.
Blau, P. M. (1963) *The Dynamics of Bureaucracy*, University of Chicago Press.
Blaxter, M. (1980) *The Meaning of Disability*, London, Heinemann.
Bocock, R. (1976) *Freud and Modern Society*, London, Thomas Nelson.
Bolger, S., Corrigan, P., Docking, J. and Frost, N. (1981) *Towards Socialist Welfare Work*, London, Macmillan.
Borkowski, M., Murch, M. and Walker, V. (1983) *Marital Violence, The Community Response*, London, Tavistock.
Brazer, G. and Holloway, S. (1978) *Changing Human Service Organizations: Policy and Practice*, New York, Free Press.
Brewer, C. and Lait, J. (1980) *Can Social Work Survive?*, London, Temple Smith.
British Association of Social Workers (1980) *Clients are Fellow Citizens*, Birmingham, BASW.
British Association of Social Workers (1977) *The Social Work Task*, Birmingham, BASW.
Brittan, A. (1973) *Meanings and Situations*, London, Routledge & Kegan Paul.
Brook, E. and Davis, A. (1985) *Women, the Family and Social Work*, London, Tavistock.
Brown, A. (1979) *Groupwork*, London, Heinemann.
Brown, G. and Harris, T. (1978) *Social Origins of Depression: A Study of Psychiatric Disorder in Women*, London, Tavistock.
Burman, S. (ed.) (1979) *Fit Work for Women*, London, Croom Helm.
Butcher, H. (1984) 'Conceptualising community social work – a response to Alan York', *British Journal of Social Work*, vol. 14, no. 6.
Butler, A. and Pritchard, C. (1983) *Social Work and Mental Illness*, London, Macmillan.
Butterworth, E. and Weir, D. (eds) (1980) *Social Problems of Modern Britain*, London, Fontana.
Carlen, P. (1983) *Women's Imprisonment: A Study in Social Control*, London, Routledge & Kegan Paul.
Cartwright, D. and Zander, A. (eds) (1968) *Group Dynamics: Research and Theory*, London, Tavistock.
Castles, F. G., Murray, D. J., Potter D. C. and Pollitt, C. J. (eds) (1978) *Decisions, Organisations and Society*, Harmondsworth, Penguin.

Central Council for Education and Training in Social Work (1977) 'Expectations of the teaching of social work in courses leading to CQSW', Consultative Document 3, London.

Cheetham, J. (ed.) (1982) *Social Work and Ethnicity*, London, George Allen & Unwin.

Clarke, J. (1979) 'Critical sociology and radical social work: problems of theory and practice', in N. Parry, M. Rustin and C. Satyamurti (eds), *Social Work, Welfare and the State*, London, Edward Arnold.

Coates, K. and Silburn, R. (1970) *Poverty: The Forgotten Englishmen*, Harmondsworth, Penguin.

Cohen, S. (1975) 'Manifestos for action', in R. Bailey and M. Brake (eds), *Radical Social Work*, London, Edward Arnold.

Cooper, D. (1971) *The Death of the Family*, Harmondsworth, Penguin.

Cornwell, J. (1984) *Hard-Earned Lives*, London, Tavistock.

Corrigan, P. and Leonard, P. (1978) *Social Work Practice under Capitalism*, London, Macmillan.

Coulson, M. and Riddell, C. (1970) *Approaching Sociology: A Critical Introduction*, London, Routledge & Kegan Paul.

Coward, R. (1983) *Patriarchal Precedents*, London, Routledge & Kegan Paul.

Craig, Y. (1977) 'The bereavement of parents and their search for meaning', *British Journal of Social Work*, vol. 7, no. 1.

Curnock, K. and Hardiker, P. (1979) *Towards Practice Theory*, London, Routledge & Kegan Paul.

Currie, R. and Parrott, B. (1981) *A Unitary Approach to Social Work: Application in Practice (an analysis of a patch system and team approach within a unitary framework in a social services department)*, Birmingham, British Association of Social Workers.

Dahrendorf, R. (1959) *Class and Class Conflict in Industrial Society*, London, Routledge & Kegan Paul.

Davies, B. (1975) *The Use of Groups in Social Work Practice*, London, Routledge & Kegan Paul.

Dobash, R. E. and Dobash, R. P. (1980) *Violence Against Wives: A Case Against the Patriarchy*, London, Open Books.

Donnison, D. (1982) *The Politics of Poverty*, Oxford, Martin Robertson.

Douglas, J. D. (1976) *Investigative Social Research*, London, Sage.

Douglas, T. (1978) *Basic Groupwork*, London, Tavistock.

Downie, R. S. and Telfer, E. (1980) *Caring and Curing*, London, Methuen.

Etzioni, A. (1964) *Modern Organisations*, New Jersey, Prentice-Hall.

Field, F. (1981) *Inequality in Britain: Freedom, Welfare and the State*, London, Fontana.

Finch, J. and Groves, D. (1980) 'Community care and the family: a case for equal opportunities', *Journal of Social Policy*, vol. 9, part 4.

Finer Report (1974) *Report of the Committee on One Parent Families*, Cmnd 5629, London, HMSO.

Fischer, J. (1973) *Interpersonal Helping: Emerging Approaches for Social Work Practice*, Springfield, Ill., Charles C. Thomas Publishers.

Fisher, M. (ed.) (1983) *Speaking of Clients*, Joint Unit for Social Services Research, Sheffield University.

Fitzherbert, K. (1967) *The West Indian Child in London*, Occasional Papers in Social Administration, London, Bell.

Fitzjohn, J. (1974) 'An interactionist view of the social work interview', *British Journal of Social Work*, vol. 4, no. 4.

Fletcher, C. (1974) *Beneath the Surface*, London, Routledge & Kegan Paul.

Fletcher, R. (1966) *The Family and Marriage*, Harmondsworth, Penguin.

Friere, P. (1973) *Education: the Practice of Freedom*, Harmondsworth, Penguin.

Fromm, E. (1968) *The Fear of Freedom*, London, Routledge & Kegan Paul.

Gammack, G. (1982) 'Social work as uncommon sense', *British Journal of Social Work*, vol. 12, no. 1.

Gammack, G. (1985) 'Split personality', *Social Work Today*, 26 August, pp. 13–15.

George, V. and Wilding, P. (1976) *Ideology and Social Welfare*, London, Routledge & Kegan Paul.

Ginsberg, N. (1979) *Class, Capital and Social Policy*, London, Macmillan.

Glastonbury, B. (1975) 'The social worker: "cannon fodder" in the Age of Admin?', *Social Work Today*, vol. 6, no. 10.

Goetschius, G. (1971) *Working with Community Groups*, London, Routledge & Kegan Paul.

Goffman, E. (1962) 'On cooling the mark out: some aspects of adaptation to failure', in A. Rose (ed.), *Human Behaviour and Social Processes*, London, Routledge & Kegan Paul.

Goffman, E. (1969) *Asylums*, Harmondsworth, Penguin.

Goldberg, E. M. (1974) 'Dilemmas in social work', *Journal of Psychosomatic Research*, vol. 18.

Goldberg, E. M. *et. al.* (1977) 'Towards accountability in social work: one year's intake to an area office', *British Journal of Social Work*, vol. 7, no. 3.

Goode, W. J. (1971) 'Force and violence in the family', *Journal of Marriage and the Family*, vol. 33, no. 4.

Gouldner, A. (1970) *The Coming Crisis of Western Sociology*, London, Heinemann.

Habermas, J. (1972) *Knowledge and Human Interests*, London, Heinemann.

Hadley, R. and Hatch, S. (1981) *Social Welfare and the Failure of the State*, London, Allen & Unwin.

Hadley, R. and McGrath, M. (1981) 'Patch systems in SSDs: more than a passing fashion', *Social Work Service*, no. 26, May.

Hadley, R. and McGrath, M. (1981) *Going Local*, NCVO Occasional Paper no. 1, London, Bedford Square Press.

Hall, A. S. (1974) *The Point of Entry*, London, George Allen & Unwin.

Hankinson, I. and Stephens, D. (1984) 'Structured IT groupwork', *Probation Journal*, vol. 31, no. 1.

Hardiker, P. (1981) 'Heart or head: the function and role of knowledge in social work', *Issues in Social Work Education*, vol. 1, no. 2.

Hardiker, P. and Barker, M. (eds) (1981) *Theories of Practice in Social Work*, London, Academic Press.

Harrison, P. (1983) *Inside the Inner City*, Harmondsworth, Penguin.

Heap, K. (1985) *The Practice of Social Work with Groups*, London, George Allen and Unwin.

Henderson, P. and Scott, T. (1984) *Learning more about Community Social Work*, London, National Institute for Social Work.

Heraud, B. (1970) *Sociology and Social Work*, Oxford, Pergamon Press.

Heraud, B. (1979) *Sociology in the Professions*, London, Open Books.

Hill, M. (1982) 'Professions in community care', in A. Walker (ed.), *Community Care: The Family, the State and Social Policy*, Oxford, Blackwell and Martin Robertson.

Hoffman, L. (1981) *Foundations of Family Therapy*, New York, Basic Books.

Holman, R. (1978) *Poverty*, Oxford, Martin Robertson.

Hopkins, J. (1982) 'What heart may warm us?', *Social Work Today*, vol. 13, no. 32.

Hopkins, J. (1984) 'Easing loneliness by social care', *Social Work Today*, vol. 16, no. 9, 29 October.

Hopson, B. (1976) 'Personal re-evaluation: a method for individual goal setting', in J. Adams, J. Hayes and B. Hopson, *Transition*, Oxford, Martin Robertson.

Howe, D. (1980) 'Inflated states and empty theories in social work', *British Journal of Social Work*, vol. 10 no. 3.

Hudson, J. (1979) 'Creating a true whole', *Social Work Today*, vol. 10, no. 48, 14 August.

Ingleby Report (1960) *Report of the Committee on Children and Young Persons*, Cmnd 1191, London, HMSO.

Irwin, J. (1970) *The Felon*, Englewood Cliffs, N.J., Prentice-Hall.

Jeffrey, M. (1976) 'Practical ways to change parent–child interaction in families of children at risk', in R. E. Helfer and C. H. Kempe (eds), *Child Abuse and Neglect: The Family and the Community*, Cambridge, Mass., Ballinger.

Johnson, T. J. (1972) *Professions and Power*, London, Macmillan.

Jones, C. (1983) *State, Social Work and the Working Class*, London, Macmillan.

Jones, K., Brown, J. and Bradshaw, J. (1983) *Issues in Social Policy*, London, Routledge & Kegan Paul.

Katz, D. and Kahn, R. L. (1970) 'Open systems theory', in O. Grusky and G. A. Miller (eds), *The Sociology of Organisations*, London, Free Press.

Kempe, R. and Kempe, C. H. (1978) *Child Abuse*, London, Fontana–Open Books.

Kincaid, J. C. (1973) *Poverty and Equality in Britain: A Study of Social Security and Taxation*, Harmondsworth, Penguin.

Laing, R. D. (1976) *The Politics of the Family*, Harmondsworth, Penguin.

Land, H. (1978) 'Who cares for the family?', *Journal of Social Policy*, vol. 7, no. 3.

Leach, E. (1967) *A Runaway World*, London, BBC Publications.

Lee, P. (1982) 'Some contemporary and perennial problems of relating theory to practice in social work', in R. Bailey and P. Lee (eds), *Theory and Practice in Social Work*, Oxford, Blackwell.

Leonard, P. (1966) *Sociology in Social Work*, London, Routledge & Kegan Paul.

Leonard, P. (1973) 'Professionalisation, community action and the growth of social services bureaucracies', in P. Halmos (ed.), *Sociological Review Monograph*, no. 20, University of Keele.

Lipset, S. M. (1963) 'Working-class authoritarianism', in S. M. Lipset (ed.), *Political Man: The Social Bases of Politics*, New York, Anchor Books.

Loewenstein, C. (1974) 'An intake team in action in a social services department', *British Journal of Social Work*, vol. 4, no. 2.

Lyons, R. (1982) 'The meaning of team and teamwork', in J. Cypher (ed.), *Team Leadership in the Social Services*, Birmingham, British Association of Social Workers.

Maslow, A. (1970) *Motivation and Personality*, New York, Harper & Row.

Marsden, D. (1969) *Mothers Alone*, Harmondsworth, Penguin.

Mathews, M. A. (1981) *The Social Work Mystique*, Washington, D.C., University Press of America.

Mathieson, T. (1974) *The Politics of Abolition*, Oxford, Martin Robertson.

Mayer, J. and Timms, N. (1970) *The Client Speaks*, London, Routledge & Kegan Paul.

McCallister, L. and Fischer, C. S. (1978) 'A procedure for surveying personal networks', *Sociological Methods and Research*, no. 7.

McKay, A., Goldberg, E. M. and Fruin, D. F., 'Consumers and a social service department', *Social Work Today*, vol. 14, no. 16.

McKinley, D. G. (1964) *Social Class and Family Life*, New York, Free Press.

Merton, R. K. (1975) 'Structural analysis in sociology', in P. M. Blau (ed.), *Approaches to the Study of Social Structure*, Free Press, 1975.

Meyer, C. (1976) *Social Work Practice – The Changing Landscape*, Free Press.

Meyer, M. W. (1979) *Change in Public Bureaucracies*, Cambridge University Press.

Miller, E. and Gwynne, G. (1971) *A Life Apart*, London, Tavistock.

Mills, C. W. (1978) *The Sociological Imagination*, Harmondsworth, Penguin.

Mills, T. M. (1967) *The Sociology of Small Groups*, New Jersey, Prentice-Hall.

Minuchin, S. (1974) *Families and Family Therapy*, Cambridge, Mass., Harvard University Press.

Mitchell, J. (1975) *Psychoanalysis and Feminism*, Harmondsworth, Penguin.

Moore, J. (1984) 'None so blind . . .', *Community Care*, no. 509, 26 April.

Morgan, D. H. J. (1985) *The Family, Politics and Social Theory*, London, Routledge & Kegan Paul.

Mullender, A. and Ward, D. (1985) 'Towards an alternative model of social group work', *British Journal of Social Work*, vol. 15, no. 2.

Murgatroyd, S. and Woolfe, R. (1985) *Helping Families in Distress*, New York, Harper & Row.

Nicolson, P. and Bayne, R. (1984) *Applied Psychology for Social Workers*, London, Macmillan.

Olsen, R. (ed.) (1979) *The Care of the Mentally Disordered: an Examination of Some Alternatives to Hospital Care*, Birmingham, British Association of Social Workers.

Owen, C. (1968) *Social Stratification*, London, Routledge & Kegan Paul.

Parry, N., Rustin, M. and Satyamurti, C. (1979) *Social Work, Welfare and the State*, London, Edward Arnold.

Parsons, T. (1961) *The Structure of Social Action*, New York, Free Press.

Parsons, T. (1970) 'Social systems', in O. Grusky and G. A. Miller (eds), *The Sociology of Organisations*, New York, Free Press.

Parsons, T. and Shils, E. A. (eds) (1951) *Towards a General Theory of Action*, Harvard University Press.

Paykel, E. S., Emms, E. M., Fletcher, J. and Rassaby, E. S. (1980) 'Life events and social support in puerperal depression', *British Journal of Psychiatry*, no. 136.

Payne, M. (1979) *Power, Authority and Responsibility in Social Services*, London, Macmillan.

Payne, M. (1982) *Working in Teams*, London, Macmillan.

Pearson, G. (1975) 'The politics of uncertainty: a study in the socialisation of the social worker', in H. Jones (ed.) *Towards a New Social Work*, London, Routledge & Kegan Paul.

Perlman, H. H. (1968) *Persona: Social Role and Personality*, University of Chicago Press.

Pizzey, E. (1974) *Scream Quietly or the Neighbours Will Hear*, Harmondsworth, Penguin.

Polansky, N. (1980) *On Loneliness: A Program for Social Work*, Studies in Social Work, New York, Smith College.

Porter, R. (ed.) (1984) *Child Sexual Abuse Within the Family*, The CIBA Foundation, London, Tavistock.

Prodgers, A. (1979) 'Defences against stress in intake work', *Social Work Today*, vol. 11, no. 2.

Ragg, N. (1977) *People Not Cases*, London, Routledge & Kegan Paul.

Randall, V. and Southgate, J. (1981) 'Creative and destructive forces in groups and organisations', *Group Relations*, June.

Randall, V. (1982) *Women and Politics*, London, Macmillan.

Rees, S. (1973) 'Clients' perspectives on social work services', unpublished paper, University of Aberdeen.

Rees, S. J. (1978) *Social Work Face to Face*, London, Edward Arnold.

Reid, W. and Shapiro, B. (1969) 'Client reactions on advice', *Social Service Review*, vol. 43, no. 2.

Rex, J. (1974) *Approaches to Sociology*, London, Routledge & Kegan Paul.

Robinson, W. P. (1972) *Language and Social Behaviour*, Harmondsworth, Penguin.

148   References and Bibliography

Rotenberg, M. (1975) 'Self labelling theory: preliminary findings among mental patients', *British Journal of Criminology*, vol. 15.

Rowan, J. (1976) *The Power of the Group*, London, Davis-Poynter.

Ruddock, R. (1969) *Roles and Relationships*, London, Routledge & Kegan Paul.

Saifullah Khan, V. (ed.) (1979) *Minority Families in Britain*, London, Macmillan.

Sainsbury, E. (1975) *Social Work with Families*, London, Routledge & Kegan Paul.

Sainsbury, E. (1982) 'Knowledge, skills and values', in R. Bailey and P. Lee (eds), *Theory and Practice in Social Work*, Oxford, Blackwell.

Satyamurti, C. (1981) *Occupational Survival*, Oxford, Blackwell.

Scanzoni, J. (1972) *Sexual Bargaining*, New York, Prentice-Hall.

Schon, D. (1971) *Beyond the Stable State*, Harmondsworth, Penguin.

Seebohm Report (1968) *Report on Local Authority and Allied Personal Social Services*, Cmnd 3703, London, HMSO.

Sheldon, B. (1978) 'Theory and practice in social work: a re-examination of a tenuous relationship', *British Journal of Social Work*, vol. 8, no. 1.

Sheppard, M. G. (1984) 'Notes on the use of social explanation to social work', *Issues in Social Work Education*, vol. 4, no. 1.

Sibeon, R. (1982) 'Theory-practice symbolisations', *Issues in Social Work Education*, vol. 2, no. 2.

Siporin, M. (1975) *Introduction to Social Work Practice*, London, Collier-Macmillan.

Smith, C. R. (1975) 'Bereavement: the contribution of phenomenological and existential analysis to a greater understanding of the problem', *British Journal of Social Work*, vol. 5, no. 1.

Smith, C. R. (1982) *Social Work with the Dying and Bereaved*, London, Macmillan.

Smith, G. (1970) *Social Work and the Sociology of Organisations*, London, Routledge & Kegan Paul.

Smith, G. and Harris, R. (1972) 'Ideologies of need and the organisation of social work departments', *British Journal of Social Work*, vol. 2, no. 1.

Smith, J. (1979) 'The social services and the inner city', in M. Loney and M. Allen (eds), *The Crisis of the Inner City*, London, Macmillan.

Statham, D. (1978) *Radicals in Social Work*, London, Routledge & Kegan Paul.

Stevenson, O. (1976) 'Social work, the courses and the local authorities', paper to the Association of Teachers in Social Work Education.

Stevenson, O. and Parsloe, P. (1979) *Social Service Teams: The Practitioners' View*, London, HMSO.

Tallman, I. (1976) *Passion, Action and Politics*, San Francisco Calif., Freeman.

Taylor, R. D. W., Huxley, P. J. and Johnson, D. A. W. (1984) 'The role of social networks in the maintenance of schizophrenic patients', *British Journal of Social Work*, vol. 14, no. 2.

Taylor, R. D. W. and Huxley, P. J. (1984) 'Social networks and support in social work', *Social Work Education*, vol. 3, no. 2.

Thomas, W. I. (1966) *On Social Organisation and Social Personality*, selected papers, M. Janowitz (ed.), Univesity of Chicago Press.

Thorpe, R. and Petruchera, J. (1985) *Community Work or Social Change?*, London, Routledge & Kegan Paul.

Timms, N. and Timms, R. (1977) *Perspectives in Social Work*, London, Routledge & Kegan Paul.

Townsend, P. (1979) *Poverty in the United Kingdom*, Harmondsworth, Penguin.

Turner, M. (1984) 'Arriving where we started: learning about failure in social work', *Issues in Social Work Education*, vol. 4, no. 1.

Twelvetrees, A. (1982) *Community Work*, London, Macmillan.

Walker, A. (ed.) (1982) *Community Care. The Family, The State and Social Policy*, Oxford, Blackwell and Martin Robertson.

Walker, H. and Beaumont, B. (1981) *Probation Work: Critical Theory and Socialist Practice*, Oxford, Blackwell.

Walton, R. (1982) *Social Work 2000*, Harlow, Longman.

Warham, J. (1977) *An Open Case*, London, Routledge & Kegan Paul.

Whitaker, D. S. (1976) 'Some conditions for effective work with groups', *British Journal of Social Work*, vol. 5, no. 4.

Whitaker, D. S. (1985) *Using Groups to Help People*, London, Routledge & Kegan Paul.

Whittaker, J. K. and Garbarino, J. (eds) (1983) *Social Support Networks – Informal Helping in the Human Services*, New York, Aldine.

Whittington, C. and Holland, R. (1981) 'Social theory and social work: teaching sociology to social workers', *Social Work Education*, vol. 1, no. 1.

Whittington, C. and Holland, R. (1985) 'A framework for theory in social work', *Issues in Social Work Education*, vol. 5, no. 6.

Wilding, P. (1981) *Socialism and Professionalism*, Tract no. 473, London, The Fabian Society.

Wilding, P. (1981) *Professional Power and Social Welfare*, London, Routledge & Kegan Paul.

Wilkes, R. (1981) *Social Work with Under-Valued Groups*, London, Tavistock.

Williams, R. (1983) *Keywords*, London, Fontana.

Wolin, S. 'Paradigms and political theories', in P. King and B. C. Parekh (eds) (1968) *Politics and Experience*, Cambridge University Press.

Worsley, P. (1976) *Introducing Sociology*, Harmondsworth, Penguin.

Worsley, P. (ed.) (1981) *Problems of Modern Society*, Harmondsworth, Penguin.

Wrong, D. H. (1961) 'The oversocialised conception of man in modern sociology', *American Sociological Review*, vol. 26, no. 2.

Younghusband Report (1959) *Report of the Working Party on Social Workers in Local Authority Health and Welfare Services*, London, HMSO.

Zimmerman, D. H. (1971) 'The practicalities of rule use', in J. D. Douglas (ed.), *Understanding Everyday Life*, London, Routledge & Kegan Paul.

Index

156   *Index*